Narcissistic Abuse Recovery

The Ultimate Guide To Understanding Narcissism And Healing From Narcissistic Lovers, Mothers And Everything In Between By Disarming The Narcissist

Chloe Hargreaves

"Healing is not an overnight process. It is a daily cleansing of pain; it is a daily healing of your life."

Leon Brown

Table of Contents

Chapter 01: Introduction

A few years back, I decided to embark on a journey that would ultimately change my life. I signed up to get professional therapy and joined a small forum that was recommended to me where survivors of psychological abuse gathered to support each other. This was a big move for me and somewhat awkward at first because I couldn't tell how this would enable me to get rid of the depression, low self-esteem and cycles of pain that I was going through. But the therapist that was treating me suggested it and quite frankly I was desperate to have a fresh start in life.

You see my story, like so many other survivors, was full of hidden psychological hurts. I realized I was carrying on a generational legacy of psychological abuse that was being passed down from generation to generation for who knows how long. The concept of love that I grew up with and experienced with my parents led me into intimate relationships and friendships that only perpetuated psychological abuse.

I had a father who was a cold, calculating control freak, and nothing I did was ever good enough for him. My mother, on the other hand, was always too warm, giving, needy, shy, and "too sensitive" according to my dad. He would often swap between mocking his wife's sensitivities my sub-par qualities. Even when I thought I had done really well (for example when I got a medal in a swimming competition), he still had countless of reasons to explain how I didn't live up to what he expected of me. My mother tried to leave my father at one point but soon got sucked back into the marriage. I even recall a time where they were sleeping in two separate bedrooms and was pretty sure it was the end of the marriage. No words were exchanged for weeks, and then slowly, my mother started exchanging warm, affectionate giggles. She got a new watch, started doing date nights again and the rest was history.

For a while, I thought this was the norm for all families. But as I grew into my teens, it started becoming even more evident that my family was very dysfunctional, and there was nothing healthy about the parental care I had received.

Each time I would start a romantic relationship, it wouldn't be too long before I found myself feeling like a human yo-yo. To my family members, I was more like the human punching bag that everyone enjoyed playing with, and even though I always felt something was off, it wasn't until my mid-twenties where I finally had enough. At first, the few people I confided in only made me feel worse - like I was paranoid, needy, and overthinking things. Perhaps you've experienced something similar?

It's tough to explain something in words that most people can barely resonate with because unless you have specific terms to describe the actions of a hidden abuser, most people will say you sound a bit crazy and unstable. Which is why I decided to do some Google research and eventually landed on a site that helped me get some professional help. Along that harrowing and intense journey, I learned some eye-opening truths about psychological abuse, which led me to the creation of this book.

As I continue to journey in life as a survivor and educate myself on this topic, it is my intention that the information I share with others can better empower them to step into their own power and heal their lives permanently.

Whether your hidden abuse comes from a romantic relationship, parents, in-laws, an employer, or whatever else the case might be for you, know that you are in the right place. Take the information contained in this book and apply it compassionately and diligently for it is the guidebook that can lead you to a life of freedom, empowerment, and self-worth.

What to expect

Abuse can take many forms. This includes mental, physical, sexual, financial, emotional, and even spiritual abuse. Most types of abuse are invisible, but they leave long-lasting scars on the survivors and deep wounds on the victims. What I am going to focus on mostly is providing you with a wealth of information on narcissistic abuse. But what's essential for you to note is that gathering the knowledge alone will not help you heal. Healing is about gaining awareness and then taking action on the acquired knowledge.

This book is specifically designed to help you reclaim your personal power so you can permanently heal. It will empower you to take full responsibility for your life and to change the current perception you carry of yourself.

You'll be able to design a life of meaning for yourself and finally be free of the past that has chained you for so long. There's a continued progression of going from the feeling of powerlessness, which is where we all start to a sense of purpose and personal power. As you go through chapter-by-chapter, that is the journey we'll be taking together, so pace yourself and start expecting the new, bolder and empowered you to emerge.

The big promise

The promise from me to you is that if you choose to walk this journey of healing with me and consume and implement all that I am sharing, you will heal and transform your life. You will be able to clearly identify, build a support system, and learn how to strengthen and protect yourself.

As I said before, my journey hasn't been easy, and it took me years to realize the real reasons behind the poor quality of life I was living. Once I realized that I was a victim, I made it my mission to make a change. I decided it must end with me.

My hope for you is that you will experience the same transformation and finally step into a greater experience of life, relationships, and love. I know it's not easy, but if you commit to taking this journey, you will come out victorious. Trust in the process and be willing to receive the new so that the old reality can become obsolete. If you're ready to begin the journey of self-healing, turn to the next chapter.

How to prepare to break free and heal from narcissistic abuse.

Depending on where you gather your information, you'll hear some people say healing takes just a few minutes while others say it will take at least a decade.

How long does it actually take to heal and recover from narcissistic abuse?

I don't have a definitive answer for you.

But wait, isn't this about healing and narcissistic abuse recovery?

Absolutely. That remains our main objective throughout this book, but sadly, what most people want is a magical silver bullet that will solve everything, and unfortunately, that doesn't exist.

The truth is, healing is a very personal thing. It is a journey, and each person will experience his or her recovery and restoration uniquely. While I cannot tell you exactly how long it will take to heal your specific situation, I can offer you six essential steps that will set a foundation for healing and help you step into this journey fully prepared to win. Failure to prepare yourself and lay down this foundation will lead to a lengthy process and might even cause you to fall off the wagon. To ensure you don't self-sabotage your own healing, do these five things:

1. Responsibility.

This is perhaps one of the most important things you will ever do in your life. Search through the rubble of your past, gather up what you need or want to keep and own it. Then tend to your wounds and find healthy ways to soothe yourself into full recovery. You are the victim of narcissistic abuse, but the only way to free yourself from that reality is to take full responsibility for your life and step out of victim mentality. You need to step up and become the King or Queen of your kingdom (so to speak) instead of allowing someone else to sit on the throne. Through this process of taking personal responsibility for how you feel, what you allow into your life and what you accept as true for you, it'll become easier to set healthy boundaries because you'll know exactly where to draw the line.

You will determine what treatment or behavior from another is acceptable to you and what you won't tolerate. At some point during your recovery, you'll see why boundaries and personal responsibility are imperative. It will start becoming evident to you that if you'd had these boundaries earlier on, or if you had begun taking full responsibility for your life earlier on, that last relationship with your ex wouldn't have landed you in another toxic experience. Your boundaries would have bounced that ex right out of your life, and it wouldn't have taken much effort from you. The web of lies, manipulation, and gaslighting wouldn't have worked on you as well, and you'd have spotted the repeat of this cycle long before it hurt you.

So what I want you to do now is to decide what boundaries you want to start implementing in your life. I also want you to make a decision that you are the sole owner of your life and that no one is responsible for your happiness, wellbeing, or success in life. Let your personal boundaries be an expression and extension of who you really believe you are. Define them and let them help you find your way back to the real and powerful you.

2. Commitment.

Make a commitment to yourself that you will no longer avoid or shy away from facing things as they are and making them better for yourself. The brain and body like to play all kinds of tricks on us, especially when we are leaving a dysfunctional relationship. As crazy as it sounds, victims tend to cling on to the very source of their trauma, especially when they believe it will take too long to heal or that it's too painful. This is referred to as a trauma bond (a bond usually established within the relationship as well as a biochemical addiction that forms in this environment).

Looking back at the early phases of your relationship where you were love bombed makes committing to this new life really hard for your brain to process because, on the one hand, you feel good thinking about this person.

But deep down, you also know the heartache and pain they cause.

Commit that you are going to move forward and never look back; otherwise, you'll never fully recover and gain freedom from the abuse.

3. Acceptance.

Self-acceptance, acceptance of the fact that you will never be able to change or fix another person is crucial. I have met victims of narcissistic abuse who were seeking information about narcissists to try and "fix" their spouse or parent. This is all in vain.

For example, Kyle came into our healing community and said she was separated from her husband and business partner, but she was hoping to find a way to heal their marriage and help him heal his tortured soul. In her mind, the best way to save her marriage and keep her son happy was to focus on fixing the narcissistic. This is the wrong approach, and I trust that at this point, you're past this.

Accept that everyone needs to take personal responsibility for his or her life and actions. You might be the most loving, caring, kind, and wonderful partner in the world; it's still not your job to force someone to be what they aren't willing to be. Accept that you're in an unhealthy relationship, work on healing yourself, and move on.

4. Expectations.

Set realistic expectations of your recovery and the amount of time needed to heal fully. Setting wildly unrealistic recovery goals for yourself, hoping that a few meditations or a few therapy sessions will bring about quick healing is self-sabotage. Why? Because when that doesn't happen, you'll feel like a failure and create an opening for the old patterns to set in again. Like any transformation, healing is a journey of incremental success. That isn't to say you can't have a radical transformation where you suddenly recover. Perhaps it might happen for you, but get into it with a long-term view and if the miracle happens, all the better for you.

5. Understanding.

The more you can understand yourself, how the narcissist works, and how life works in general, the smoother this journey will become. I see so many aspiring survivors mistakenly believe that healing is merely getting out of the abusive relationship. Worse still, they believe reading a book, joining a forum or buying a course is enough to fix their situation. Unfortunately, this belief can keep you stuck for years if you're not careful because even if you physically leave the abusive relationship, healing requires more than just the physical act. Symptoms of trauma, depression, panic, complex grieve and anxiety are widespread among victims and aspiring survivors because they lack true understanding.

Don't get me wrong, reading, watching videos, joining a forum can be helpful, but they will not heal you. You will acquire knowledge and receive validation, but ultimately, the healing can only happen within. Your actions, the state of mind you place yourself in and the inner work you do are what will get you the results you desire.

Remember, our old mental, and emotional conditioning, trapped emotions, trauma, and patterns of thought determine our wellbeing. To truly heal, we must actively work on ourselves and gain true understanding about who we are, what our potential is, and where our real power lies.

6. Let go.

One of the hardest parts of ending any relationship is learning to let go, release, forgive, and detach. We talk more about this throughout the book, and I even help you practice the art of detachment. This is an inner shift and requires you to consciously recognize that you can make it alone; that you don't need to be defined by the narcissist or your relationship. It's about dissolving the belief that you need him or her to feel good about yourself or to be important in this world. I want you to slowly start training yourself to believe that no matter what you will be okay. It's a deep knowing that must be cultivated, and the nurturing of this knowing begins when you learn to stop attaching your identity, self-worth, and value to anything or anyone. Release the need to prove the narcissist wrong. Let go of waiting for apologies or closure and create a space for true healing within yourself that takes power off everything and everyone in your world and hands it over to you.

With these simple foundational steps, you are well on your way to true healing. But remember you must work through all five, in whatever order you prefer. To have the life of your dreams where true love, passion, freedom, and empowerment is a daily reality; you must set up a right and robust foundation.

"To live in this world, you must be able to do three things: Love what is mortal; hold it against your bones knowing your own life depends on it; and when the time comes to let it go, let it go."
- Mary Oliver.

Chapter 02: Recognizing The Abusive Narcissist

I think we can all agree that narcissism is created over a long and complicated psychological development that usually begins during childhood. While many people assume being selfish, arrogant, and attention seeking makes one a narcissist, the truth is they are not one and the same.

The great American psychologist William James believed that phenomena are best understood when placed within their series, studied in their germ and in their over-ripe decay". In the 2018 Cognitive Neuroscience of Narcissism J Brain Behav Cogn Sci Vol 1:6, I found a very enlightening resource that can help all of us better understand narcissism based off the same premise presented by William James. "If we take the phenomena of self-interest and observe it in its most germinal form, we see a

Darwinian instinct that has great survival value. Moving up the series, a more severe form of self-interest, known as selfishness produces excessive or exclusive concern with oneself. The narcissistic needs to maintain a relatively positive self-image underlies individuals' needs for validation and affirmation as well as the motivation to overtly and covertly seek out validation and self-enhancement experiences from the social environment. This need can produce selfish behaviors such as cheating and lying, which undermine the efforts of organized society. However, selfishness is not considered pathological. Self-interest reaches its 'over-ripe decay' at the point of a narcissistic personality disorder (NPD) which depicts a pathological complex that is self-reinforcing and produces harmful effects on the individual, close relationships and possibly the broader social community." (George FR, Short D 2018 The Cognitive Neuroscience of Narcissism. J Brain Behav Cogn Sci Vol 1:6)

In other words, being a narcissist, in general, isn't considered pathological. But he or she may gradually develop a disorder if the behavior is left unchecked and carried to great extremity. Narcissism is a continuum that stretches across a spectrum. It is essential to realize that not all narcissists are considered pathological by medical standards and some narcissistic qualities may actually be beneficial to have as you will learn later on, but it's still wise to educate yourself as much as possible about their general tendencies of narcissists and how to spot a malignant type.

Who or what is a narcissist?

A narcissist is a specific type of person considered to be the opposite of an empath. Dealing with a narcissist is never easy, and it's important you learn to recognize if you have one in your life so you can better protect yourself and handle those relationships appropriately. Failure to do so may actually result in unnecessary suffering and wounds that damage your quality of relationships and experience of love.

According to the American Psychological Association, personality disorders are stable maladaptive patterns of behavior that involve at least two of the following four areas: Cognitive (thought patterns), affective (emotional patterns), interpersonal (patterns of relating to others) and impulse-control-based.

There are various types of personality disorders, which create impairment in how people function in their lives. In the United States of America alone, it is reported that about ten percent of the population is affected by some form of personality disorder. But when it comes to narcissistic personality disorders, they believe that it's still very rare with about one percent of the population actually suffering from it. When it comes to recognizing narcissists in your life, understand that not everyone who has narcissistic traits can be diagnosed as having NPD. But just because it's not extreme enough to be diagnosed doesn't mean they can't harm you. Here's an abbreviated summary of the diagnostic criteria for NDP according to the latest Diagnostic and Statistical Manual of Mental Disorders (DSM-V).

• A belief that he or she is "special" and unique and can only be understood by or should associate with similar high-status people.

• A grandiose sense of self-importance.

• Highly manipulative.

• A need for excessive admiration.

• Monopolization of conversations to belittle or degrade the people they perceive as inferior.

• A tendency to use others for their own needs and wants.

• Unable to handle criticism of any kind.

• Lack of empathy and inability to recognize the needs and feelings of others.

• An exaggerated arrogance demonstrated in behavior and/ or attitude.

• Lack of remorse for hurting others and never experience guilt.

The narcissist's false self and true self:

We all have our "ego ideal" that helps us orient our goals and navigate life. When this ego ideal is pathologically distorted, it becomes the false self. In general, we all create a mental representation of the ideal state of the self, which usually possesses every perfection. In the case of narcissism, this becomes even more evident.

The underlying factors that lead to extreme personality disorder, which are frequently wounds that require healing get suppressed and layered up with a false image. This false image is the one the narcissist initially presents to you, and because they are so good at facades, it takes a while before you can start to see cracks in the mask. Because the narcissist is doing everything they can to avoid dealing with his or her unresolved wounds, they strive to find distractions and energy sources that can help them attain an ideal that they believe the real (and hidden) self is incapable of achieving. In other words, they try to live purely from the ego self and make it as powerful as possible.

To solicit attention, admiration, and get the supply he or she needs, a narcissist will flaunt a false self. He or she pretends to be all-powerful, omnipotent, unique, brilliant, and superior to you. It's good to remember that the false self in malignant narcissists is an adaptive reaction to pathological circumstances, but its dynamics make it predominant. The false self in the narcissist devours the psyche and preys upon the true self (and the inner child) of the individual. This is why such people are unable to express and portray a healthy, flexible, and holistically functioning personality.

The remnants of an authentic self are usually so shredded and repressed into submission that for all practical purposes this true self in the narcissist is rendered dysfunctional. In a malignant narcissist, the false self completely takes over and imitates the true self causing the narcissist to reinterpret certain negative emotions and reactions in a flattering socially acceptable light. For example, instead of admitting fear, the narcissist will usually try to justify how they feel in a way that solicits admiration or compassion. Malignant narcissists also emulate and fake things like compassion, empathy, affection, and so on to prey on their victims so they can create a stable source of supply that can feed the false self.

The narcissist's ego-self, which is always power hungry, can invest in physical objects or oneself to reclaim this desired ideal while muting out healthy emotional investments to reclaim that missing sense of wholeness. The possession of material objects seems to help increase self-confidence and self-esteem in the narcissist. The same thing also happens when it comes to places and people that the narcissist considers valuable. Their own sense of value and self-worth increases when they associate with such people, and as such, they go to great lengths to only associate with organizations, people, and places they consider superior.

A narcissist will only pay attention to you when he or she feels like you help them get closer to their ego ideal so whenever there's a discrepancy in your interaction with them, only negativity can result because they will feel wounded and resentful.

For example, think of a time when the narcissist in your life gave you a strange look as though you had done something wrong simply because of how intelligently you answered a question or how skillfully you executed an action. That was probably one of the first red flags that you chose to ignore because you wanted to maintain peace or because the person had been so charming otherwise. Jealousy and envy is something a narcissist will struggle with a lot because they always want to be the ones winning and performing things that others marvel at.

To a narcissist's mind, you are undermining them when you do something wonderful because your role should be something that helps them shine, not the other way around. At the start of the relationship; however, what you experience is the false mask covering the wounded ego self that they are trying to build up. The charm, thoughtfulness, attentiveness, loving, caring nature is just a facade meant to entice you into their vortex of narcissistic abuse. As long as you're the distraction that's keeping them in the calm zone, it won't be easy to unmask their ego self, and it will undoubtedly feel impossible to understand what their true self is like.

If as you go through this description, there's resonance within you, then it's probably a good thing you're here because it is time to sever the bond you have with this person. Their problematic behavior and the difficulty you have in dealing with them is good enough cause to distance yourself from such relationships. Narcissists are generally happy, far happier at least than the people in their lives because they aren't aware (or don't care) about the negative consequences of their behavior and actions. So it's highly unlikely a narcissist will agree to therapy, which can include a diagnosis.

Most people seek therapy out of discomfort and pain, which isn't usually something the narcissist will be dealing with. Although it is unethical for a trained therapist to diagnose friends and family with NPD due to potential bias and certainly not an official diagnosis for you as a layperson to view the diagnostic criteria and declare someone to have a psychological disorder, I do encourage you to educate yourself thoroughly. Get to understand the signs, observe your current situations, and the state of the relationships that bring you pain and suffering. Empower yourself with knowledge and then do something to improve your life.

Don't mind too much about forcing a narcissist to get help once you recognize you're in a relationship with one. Instead, work on your self-healing and building a new lifestyle that frees you from that relationship.

In the next chapter we will be diving deeper into the different types of narcissists you need to become aware of and some of the traits they possess but before then, let's shed some light on what narcissistic abuse is and some of the ways it may present itself.

What is narcissistic abuse?

Narcissistic abuse is a term coined by Sam Vaknin that refers to any kind of abuse by a narcissist. Typically emotional abuse, it often occurs in adult-adult relationships or parent-child relationships.

To fully comprehend what narcissistic abuse is we need to view it as a spectrum with varying degrees. It stretches from ignoring your feelings to violent outbursts of rage, aggression, and everything in between.

Few narcissists will self-reflect and even feel guilty of their actions when they mistreat you so as a general rule, don't expect them to take responsibility for their behavior. According to some studies, an adult who experiences a relationship with a narcissist will tend to struggle with knowing what true love (or a healthy relationship) is. There's also a tendency for children who grow up with narcissists to become victims of narcissistic abuse in their adult years.

Different types of abuse to become aware of:

• Verbal abuse - this includes shaming, criticizing, sarcasm, bullying, threatening, undermining, interrupting, and name-calling.

• Manipulation - this of usually an expression of covert aggression.

• Negative contrasting - this is often when the narcissist is unnecessarily comparing you with others in a negative way.

• Lying - this involves persistent deception to avoid responsibility or to achieve the narcissist's own needs.

• Neglect - this consists of ignoring the needs of a partner or a child. In the case of narcissistic parents, it includes child endangerment such as leaving a child in dangerous situations.

• Sabotage - this involves disruptive interference with your endeavors for personal advantage or for revenge.

• Withholding - this includes keeping things such as money, sex, or affection from you.

Can empaths be narcissists too?

The first time I asked this question in my online community for healing survivors, I was met with a lot of resistance. I mean empaths are supposed to be the opposites of narcissists, right?

Well, here's the thing. Being an empath doesn't automatically mean you always feel empathy toward others, and being a narcissist doesn't mean you are utterly incapable of feeling what others feel.

We tend to make it a black and white scenario, which isn't exactly right. Most of us only perceive narcissists as obnoxious extroverted self-obsessed people. Think most Hollywood celebrities.

But did you know there are overt and covert narcissists?

Overt narcissists are habitually thick-skinned and openly conceited.

Covert narcissists are usually shy, sensitive, and introverted. It's crucial you learn to recognize the signs and traits as both types possess similar characteristics, but of course, the covert will be way harder to spot. In fact, many times, they may mask themselves as empaths.

I have a friend who finally confessed to this discovery in his own life. For years he firmly believed that he was an empath. He created an idealized self-image that masked the fact that underneath he was actually a wounded, self-centered egomaniac who couldn't truly empathize. He tended to shift from acting superior to others and feeling hurt by them. He always felt victimized by life and other people.

One of the key insights he discovered while going through the self-healing journey was that within him was the darkness that was being masked by his empathic self-image. His sensitive, vulnerable, and introverted nature did not cancel out his narcissistic tendencies. For years he struggled with this feeling that he was a victim of everyone else's feelings and thoughts. And even though he felt other people's pain so strongly, he had little understanding toward them.

What this taught me is that even with empaths, it is possible to have underlying wounds that need healing. One becomes a narcissistic empath when he or she denies or avoids the feeling of vulnerability that comes with that level of sensitivity, and of course, this stems from having low self-esteem. Narcissistic empaths are too concerned about protecting themselves that they shut out their ability to genuinely care for others.

This question "can empaths be narcissists" cannot have a straight yes or no answer. It's obviously up for considerable debate, and I'm sure you'll have your opinion as well, but I encourage you to keep an open mind and be on the lookout for certain common symptoms that non-regular narcissists would tend to demonstrate. Here are a few:

• Feeling fundamentally different from others and more unique.

• Perceiving others in extremes and being overly judgmental. For example, demonizing a person.

• Self-martyrdom as a way of manipulating and controlling others.

• Finger pointing and a tendency to blame others instead of taking responsibility for their actions and feelings.

• Intensely offended by any sign of criticism.

Chapter 03: What You May Not Know About Narcissism and NPD

First of all, let's break an old myth that usually confuses a lot of people. Narcissism is not all negative. There is a difference between healthy narcissism and narcissistic abuse. According to psychologist Dr. Susan Kolod, everyone needs to practice a good dose of healthy narcissism. The diagnosis of narcissistic personality disorder is indeed very negative and includes characteristics such as arrogance, preoccupation with oneself, a need for constant admiration and most importantly, a lack of empathy for others. But narcissism itself is not positive or negative - there is a continuum from healthy to pathological, Kolod says.

According to Dr. Kolod, healthy narcissism is related to self-esteem and self-worth, and it involves being able to take pleasure in one's beauty and experiencing ecstatic joy in oneself.

Why is having healthy narcissism necessary?

Well, if you can experience joy in yourself, feel proud of your accomplishment and feel worthy, then you can face many difficult challenges boldly. It can also help you experience a sense of self-satisfaction and fulfillment in your own work and the impact you have on the world. When children aren't raised in an environment that helps them develop healthy narcissism, that's when things start going wrong.

On the other hand, when one suffers from a narcissistic personality disorder, they fall into the extreme of these tendencies and develop inflated self-importance and an excessive need for attention and admiration.

The Cause Of Narcissism

As mentioned above, narcissistic tendencies are quite normal for most human beings. Think of a 2-year-old baby who is in love with the world and has just discovered "mine" and "I." The child will naturally demonstrate tendencies of narcissism and then slowly grow into an understanding that relating to others requires a shift (assuming the parents do a good job teaching this). If however, the child grows up in a dysfunctional family, then what would be a healthy sense of narcissism will likely And then we get the extreme version that often leads to narcissistic abuse. This is usually what's medically diagnosed as a personality disorder, and the root cause of all the pain, hurt, and suffering victims of narcissistic abuse have to endure. Going back to the statement offered by William James that implies every phenomenon has a point of becoming over-ripe, this point is reached when narcissistic tendencies are taken to an extreme and turn into a personality disorder. Although we cannot state with certainty what causes this, we do know three major factors act as a catalyst.

• Psychological or environmental factors
This, to me, seems to be one of the main factors that lead to NPD. It could be early childhood trauma, heartbreak, mid-life crisis, or grief. Children who lacked proper parental support and care or those shuffled between foster parents are more prone to this disorder because they usually suffer from an identity crisis.

• Biological factors
Malignant narcissism can literally be passed down from one generation to the next within a family. But we cannot attribute causation to genes alone. If narcissistic parents raised a man, and he develops similar traits, there are there biological factors that can turn him into a malignant narcissist.

First and foremost, his temperament. If he lacks emotional control and maturity and is considered quick-tempered, extravagant, attention seeking, and self-indulgent, then he can quickly develop NPD.

Second would be his neurobiology. If certain changes occur in this neurobiological system, it might influence his judgment, social skills, problem-solving skills, and the way he responds to stress in general.

Third would be a genetic influence because even though we know genes cannot be the sole reason for developing NPD, we cannot overrule its influence. According to recent research on genetics, scientists have discovered that if one monozygotic twin has a criminal background, then there's a 66% chance the other might also exhibit the same behavior, but the numbers significantly reduce to 31% chance if they are dizygotic twins.

• Social and cultural factors

Cultural confusion, unemployment, migration, media can all contribute to this disorder for a narcissist who struggles to regulate his or her emotions. Usually, malignant narcissism comes along with other psychiatric disorders such as depression, borderline, and antisocial personality disorders.

Bottom line is, malignant narcissists can be very harmful and create a lot of damage in your life if you continue hanging around them, so you need to know how to face them and escape that pit of despair and suffering.

What is NPD?

A narcissistic personality disorder is a diagnosed medical condition that turns narcissists into unhealthy, dangerous people, especially on a mental and emotional level. These people are exploitative, entitled, and lack empathy. They are so addicted to feeling special that they'll use extreme measures including stealing, cheating, sabotage, lying, or whatever else it takes to get what they want. And they have no concern or compassion for those they affect in the process.

As with all personality disorders, the exact nature of narcissistic personality disorder (NPD) cannot be drilled down to a single event. It's usually a combination of early childhood experiences, psychological factors, and sometimes even genes.

Early childhood factors include trauma, abuse, excessive criticism, extremely high expectations, and intensive parenting. It could also be a result of being hypersensitive (as in the case of empaths) and not knowing how to handle the sensitivities very well. Although the single root cause remains unknown, all professionals agree that getting treatment is vital. The sooner the treatment is given, the higher the chances of lessening or even wholly healing from the disorder.

The less commonly discussed problem is the wake of devastation that a narcissist leaves behind as they interact with people. Some cases are so server they can affect the entire future of the victim. Here's a story that a friend shared, which helps show how awful life can be for those of us subjected to narcissistic abuse.

Sarah survived decades of emotional abuse from her mother. She said everything was always blamed on her. The mother would often say, "you should have been aborted, you're poison." As she got older, her narcissistic mother started sexually shaming her by repeatedly telling her no boys would ever find her attractive because she had no breasts. Sarah said that her mother was like a vampire finding any excuse to feed on Sarah's pain and anguish. It's easy to see why the girl grew up with no self-esteem, always afraid to speak her mind or state her desires. At the age of 18, she went for an interview hoping to be hired as a tutor but the woman interviewing her was so alarmed at how insecure, jittery and shy Sarah was that she kept asking her if everything was okay.

Sarah didn't get that job, and it took a lot of work to finally get her out of that state of insecurity and feeling invisible. She confessed that she felt as though she was nothing, invaluable in the world and that she didn't feel like she had a real identity to present to the world.

Another excellent example of how narcissistic abuse presents itself in adult-to-adult relationships can be seen in Gemma's story. Gemma Matheson met Alex at a party of a Friday night having been introduced by mutual friends. They spent all evening flirting, dancing, drinking, and having a blast. By Saturday afternoon the next day, the two were a couple. Alex was a charming Real Estate agent with his sights on the top position at his company. He even had a four-year plan laid out for how he would get it. "We met Friday night, and by the following weekend, he was taking mortgages, a big wedding, and kids," says Gemma. She completely fell for him believing that finally, she had found Mr. Right. The perfect man who was in it for the long haul. Six months into the relationship and his euphoric highs and romantic gestures were countered by severe aloofness and painful rejection. "He'd invite me to dinner or a party, then cancel the offer minutes before we were due to go out and once he actually canceled a holiday hours before our flight. I thought nothing of it and soon became standard behavior because I always made allowances for these types of behaviors. Looking back, I should have known how it would all end." laments Gemma.

In spring of last year, Alex said he was planning a special surprise dinner during which time he proposed to Gemma who obviously said yes. Three days after the special dinner, Alex sent a text message terminating their relationship, and Gemma hasn't heard from him since. The mutual friend that introduced them was just as shocked and said Alex seems to be doing well but avoids talking about what happened. Each time it comes up, he simply says that he's working out some stuff and would rather not discuss it. This is a classic symptom of avoidant personality disorder combined with narcissism, and unfortunately, Gemma is left to pick up the pieces of her broken heart.

These are just a few of the countless stories that we'll often hear in our community of people who are trying to get out of or recover from narcissistic abuse. The term best used to describe those of us that suffer the consequences of narcissism is Echoism. It was first coined in a 2005 paper by psychoanalyst Dean Davis and popularized by psychologist Dr. Craig Malkin Ph.D. who wrote a book called Rethinking Narcissism.

What is echoism, and what does it have to do with narcissistic abuse?

Echoism is a trait that Dr. Malkin and his colleagues are currently studying and it's starting to gain a lot of attention, especially with survivors of narcissistic abuse. According to his research, Dr. Malkin believes it is a trait that exists in all of us. For some, it is stronger and more pronounced while in others, it's very subtle. Dr. Malkin says that people who score above average in echoism qualify as echoists and their defining characteristic is a fear of being a burden or coming across as narcissistic. Most of these people are warm-hearted and kind, but they feel uncomfortable about receiving praise and attention.

In other words, echoists, especially those who are extremely abundant with this trait, never feel special, and they suffer greatly for it. Because they don't want to be a burden or to shine, they are naturally attracted to narcissists who have no trouble grabbing the spotlight overshadowing the emotional anxiety experienced by an echoist.

Echoism arises when someone is in a toxic relationship with a narcissist.
This concept of echoism is drawn from the Greek myth of Narcissus and Echo. Narcissus is the god who became entranced by his own reflection. A familiar tale many of us have heard. What we don't usually hear is the story of Echo, the wood nymph who was cursed to near-silence and able only to repeat the last words she hears.

Echo fell in love with Narcissus, but all she could do was echo what he said. Just like Echo in Greek Mythology, echoists tend to fall into relationships with narcissists because they struggle to have a voice of their own. They become proficient at echoing the needs of the narcissist in their lives and ultimately lose their identity and self-worth. Victims of narcissistic abuse learn to bury their needs, feelings, and preferences and develop coping mechanisms to survive the relationship.

Dr. Malkin shares a very vulnerable story that helps us understand how he came up with this concept during the writing of his famous book "Rethinking Narcissism."

"As a child, I struggled to celebrate my achievements. I found reasons to dismiss praise with statements such as - the test was easy, or the teacher likes me. And I blamed myself whenever someone hurt me. I was far more comfortable providing care than receiving it. It was only many years later when I was writing Rethinking Narcissism and rereading the myth or Narcissus that I had an aha moment. Like the love-struck nymph in the myth, echoists, like myself, can echo the needs and feelings of others, but we are at a loss when it comes to 'voicing' our own desires. We play Echo to Narcissus, shrinking from the special attention that narcissists thrive on."

It's important to note here that Dr. Malkin considers echoism a trait, not a disorder and at best should be thought of as a survival strategy for those who struggle to enjoy the feeling of being special and important.

Eventually, the victims and survivors of narcissistic abuse will seek out therapy because they feel depressed, suffer from anxiety or feel like they are on the verge of going crazy even if they don't know why they feel that way. If you're reading this and recognizing your own story of abuse, know that it's not your fault and you are not alone. Help is available, and you can heal yourself from that life of devastation. The more aware you become of narcissistic behavior and traits that you possess that make you an easy target, the easier it will to spot and avoid them on your road to recovery.

There are many free websites online that offer quizzes to help you determine whether you or someone you know is exhibiting symptoms of either mild or a more severe case of narcissistic personality disorder. I encourage you to take the quiz but with the bearing in mind that it does not medically diagnose NPD.

Different types of narcissists

From a medical standpoint, there is only one diagnosis for narcissistic disorders, but within it are multiple variants and degrees of severity.

According to a 2012 review of the research on narcissism, some of these variants that were identified included grandiose narcissists, vulnerable narcissists, and malignant narcissists.

Grandiose narcissists require excessive praise and attention. Vulnerable narcissists tend to have a lot of anxiety issues and need lots of supportive attention.

Malignant narcissists are considered the most damaging of them all because beyond being overly self-focused, they tend to have a darker side to their self-absorption. This subset tends to have antisocial traits and even a sadistic streak. In fact, some experts see little difference between psychopaths and malignant narcissists because they both have a sadistic, antisocial streak with almost no empathy for others.

Our primary focus in this book is on malignant narcissists because they are the more common and most damaging types when it comes to our interaction with them. Other types may be less dangerous but certainly equally annoying and challenging to be around, but as it relates to your well-being and narcissistic abuse, malignant narcissists are definitely the ones you must become wary of.

What are some traits and symptoms of a narcissist?

It's only fair that I share with you some new research that shows there are some positive and beneficial traits that a narcissist has that could help him or her succeed in life. Researchers at Queen's University Belfast have found that narcissists possess what the researchers have dubbed as "mental toughness." An ability that propels them into success.

As much as narcissism is considered negative, some doctors are starting to believe that's it's not all bad. A lecturer at the school of psychology by the name of Dr. Kostas Papageorgiou did a study called Mental Toughness: A Personality Trait That Is Relevant Across Achievement And Mental Health Outcomes. In the study, he discovered that adolescents who display some of the traits associated with narcissism might also be more mentally tough, and because of this perform better at school. As part of the study, three hundred and forty students were recruited from three different high schools in Milan, and researchers looked to see if there was an association between mental toughness and achievement. Their findings proved that mental toughness correlated with narcissism. Dr. Papageorgiou seems to think people with narcissistic traits could actually do more good than harm if they kept themselves in check at all times. "People who score high on subclinical narcissism may be at an advantage because their heightened sense of self-worth may mean they are more motivated assertive and successful in certain contexts," said Dr. Papageorgiou.

So there's probably some positivity to being a narcissist but usually not for those around such a person. Often it is their initial positive aspect that attracts us, especially in intimate relationships. That's why before we talk about the negative traits of a malignant narcissist; I want to make you aware of some of the positive characteristics narcissists have that usually draw innocent victims into their web of devastation.

• Charismatic.

- Witty.
- Romantic.
- Ambitious.
- Attentive and affection, especially in the early stages.
- Very confident and high self-esteem.
- Persuasiveness.

Personality disorders, especially malignant narcissism, carries certain traits that are relatively easy to spot. Here are some signs to look out for:

• A heightened sense of entitlement.

A malignant narcissist always has unreasonable expectations of superior treatment. They feel entitled to have what they want when they want, as they want it, and people should automatically comply with their demands. The narcissist's world is very black and white. It's good/bad, right/wrong, superior/inferior, and he or she is always on the right side of things. Narcissists have to win all the time no matter what, and they must be the best at everything.

• Grandiosity.

Malignant narcissists, in general, believe they are superior to most people and are better than most people. A malignant narcissist takes this sense to a whole new level and actually lashes out when people don't adapt to this worldview. They believe "I am everything and you are nothing; I have everything, and you have nothing." Anyone who contradicts that viewpoint stands to suffer much, especially if the narcissists perceive the person as inferior to them.

• Egocentricity.

Narcissists have egos that are totally out of control. He or she only talks about himself or herself and continually seeks praise and compliments. In truth, they believe the world revolves around them, and everyone is there to serve their needs. The danger of being around an egocentric narcissist is that you stand to be on the receiving end of their rage if you choose to contradict their perspective or want to disagree with the way they do things.

• Perfectionism.

This is very common for most narcissists because they have an extreme need for everything to be perfect. They want to control each and every detail around them to make sure it matches the high standards they've set for themselves, and when that fails to happen, things become really bad for those around them. According to a narcissist, life should play out exactly as they envision it.

• Lack of boundaries.

A narcissistic cannot see where they end and you begin, which means as far as they are concerned, everything belongs to them, and everyone thinks, feels, and wants the same things they want. Think of a 2-year-old's behavior, and you're pretty close to understanding how a narcissist operates. If a narcissist wants something from you, he or she will go to any lengths to get it whether the means used are healthy or harmful.

• Manipulation.

It's not uncommon for all of us to try to use a situation to our advantage at times, but true manipulation runs deeper than the occasional cajoling. Real narcissists are experts at constant manipulation. They are not interested in the well-being of others and only cares about people when they can see how to use them as a vehicle to gain control, power, or profit in some way. Narcissists are so good at manipulation that they can take what you say or do and twist it around so much to the point where you start to question your own truth and reality.

• Deceitfulness.

Narcissists are usually very deceitful and regularly lie, con people, cheat and malinger just to get personal profit or pleasure. Their inability to "put themselves in another person's shoes" makes it easy for them to lie without any guilty conscience. The most important thing for them is that they come out looking good and in possession of what they desire. Sometimes they will use rationalization to twist words in their favor, which can make it difficult for the victim to figure out what is real and what is false about the narcissist's behavior.

• Lack of empathy.

Narcissists are unable to feel and empathize with the experience of another. They cannot process emotions the same we the rest of us do, which also means they usually don't experience the same sensation of guilt or remorse an average person would if they acted poorly. Due to the fact that narcissists cannot comprehend what other people are feeling, it's hard for them to see their actions as wrong and in fact, many believe that they are the victims of criticism and mistreatment.

• Sadistic and cruel.

Narcissists, especially malignant narcissists, tend to enjoy inflicting pain. They possess this sadistic quality that promotes taking advantage of people, inflicting harm, and humiliation.

• Inexplicable Hatred and anger.

Most malignant narcissists carry a lot of rage and anger without reason, and those around them tend to be on the receiving end of these negative emotions, which creates emotional abuse. When exposed to such a person as a child or adult, it's easy to blame yourself and internalize the rage and hatred you experience, which becomes very damaging. But there is never a logical reason, and it's not your fault when the narcissists act out in this way.

• Paranoia.

Although many people experience some level of paranoia, it doesn't occur as often or as intensely as it does with a malignant narcissist. He or she will over analyze everything people say and approach all people with suspicion and criticism even though they don't like to receive any form of criticism. For example, if someone happens to bump into a malignant narcissist at the bar, the narcissists will view this as something intentionally done to cause them harm in some way even if it was just a pure accident. They are especially paranoid that other people may be trying to take away their power, possessions, or harm them in some twisted way.

• **Projection.**

This usually happens when the narcissist projects their behavior onto someone else mostly because they are unwilling to see their own shortcomings. The malignant narcissists may know of his or her shortcomings but rather than admit them, they prefer to deflect and insist that the rest of the world is guilty of doing what they are doing. This is why you'll find many malignant narcissists claiming that they are the victims being mistreated and so the real victims of narcissistic abuse end up feeling like everything is their fault.

• **Fear.**

A narcissist is strongly motivated by fear, but much of the time, these fears are deeply buried and repressed, making it hard to spot them. The main reason narcissists cannot take any criticism, rejection, or ridicule is because of this deeply hidden fear. If you're observant, you can see this fear surfacing, especially when the narcissist feels threatens or if they believe someone is out to get their power, status, money, etc. Most narcissists fear being vulnerable or having real intimacy with anyone because they are afraid you will see their inadequacies and imperfections and judge or reject them.

I have realized its almost impossible for narcissists to develop real trust and love of others because the deep-seated fear controlling their lives is always in control, so they do everything possible to mask it because they don't want to be found out or abandoned by the people around them.

This is list is far from exhausted, and with a little more research I'm sure you'll find lots more signs and symptoms that can help you understand whether you're dealing with a malignant narcissist or not. Aside from the symptoms, there are also varying levels of narcissism you must become aware of.

Types of extreme narcissists

Narcissism occurs along a continuum of expression that ranges from healthy to unhealthy, as I mentioned in an earlier chapter. Here are a few types you might easily encounter in our modern society.

• The bullying narcissist

This type of person builds himself or herself by humiliating other people. The example I shared about Sarah and her mother is a perfect example of a bullying narcissist, and such a person tends to be very brutal about the way they assert their superiority.

He or she will belittle and mock you, make you feel like you are nothing, and have no value. Such a person makes you doubt yourself and your value as a human being.

• The seductive narcissist

Unlike many of the extreme narcissists, this type of person actually manipulates you by making you feel good about yourself. At first, he or she idolizes and offers lots of admiration, but the ultimate goal is to use you in some way. Such a person craves support and admiration and will use flattery and seduction to get it, but when they get to a point where they have no further use for you, all you'll get is a cold shoulder.

• The Vindictive Narcissist

This type of narcissism can be very damaging to your life. He or she is very much into revenge and getting back at you. At work, they might try to get you fired, or if it's an ex-wife, she might do everything in her power to turn the kids against you. Such a person knows no limits when it comes to getting back at people they believe have wronged them in some way.

• The grandiose narcissist

This type of person is quite common in today's world. We can easily recognize him or her. Such a person believes they are more important, influential, and superior than others. They love showing off their accomplishments and always exaggerate their importance in an attempt to gain more admiration or make others envious. This type of narcissist truly believes they are destined for great things and as a matter of fact, can accomplish a lot and succeed in the business world due to their overgrown ambitions.

• The know-it-all

This type of narcissists is the one we all found annoying in school. Always eager to give their opinion even when no one asked and believes they know everything. He or she likes to argue, lecture, and condescending people and struggles to listen because they are always so self-absorbed. Instead of genuinely listening to you, they would be busy thinking about what they'd like to say next. Although not as damaging as the previously mentioned types, it's still good to be on the lookout and to avoid these types of people.

Traits of perfect targets for narcissists

Some people find themselves in a narcissistic relationship, break their way out, and spend the rest of their lives avoiding narcissists. Then there are those of us who just seem to be magnets for narcissists.

We dig ourselves out of one relationship with a narcissist only to find ourselves trapped in a new one.

A friend of mine spent years clawing her way out of narcissistic abuse with her dad, and a few years later, she was in a new abusive situation. Regardless of which one hits close to home for you know that there is nothing wrong with you. There is, however, an active tendency in you to attract narcissists, perhaps due to certain qualities you possess, and it's imperative you increase your awareness.

Certain personality types and characteristics are very appealing to narcissists, and it's crucial you get to learn more about yourself so you can see why they seem to "prey" on you or why you have a tendency of falling victim to a narcissist.

Narcissists, especially those that are malignant are good at carefully choosing, charming, seducing, and trapping a victim. Your energy is then used to feed him or her. It's what gives the narcissist a foot in the door to carry out their manipulation tactics and devastate your life.

- You are highly sensitive to other people's feelings, and you love unconditionally.

Don't get me wrong here, this is one of your greatest strengths, and loving people unconditionally is supposed to be a wonderful thing in an ideal world. Unfortunately, when it comes to narcissists, this quality makes you a magnet for them because when he or she understands this about you and exploiting that gift will be the natural impulse.

You may have experienced moments where your abuser apologizes, starts crying or showers you with praise only to plunge you back into that feeling of worthlessness. They usually create this facade to make us believe that they love us and they use it to keep us hooked until the next outburst so don't fall for this trick anymore.

- You're always reliable, dependable, and ready to help others.

If you tend to keep a low profile and have no wish to overshadow the people in your life, then a narcissist sees this as a perfect opportunity to trap you in their web of lies.

• You have a natural desire to heal others
This applies a lot to empaths, which is probably why they are the biggest magnets for narcissists. If you feel everyone in the world needs to be loved and that given the right environment and attention anyone can change then you'll naturally feel attracted to a narcissist. Something in you will always want to heal and fix narcissists because you believe they can turn themselves around and stop hurting people. The narcissists will naturally feel attracted to you and will be more than happy to cling to you for dear life.

When a narcissist knows you will never turn down their fight and that you're emotionally attached to them, manipulating you for personal gain becomes the game to play and trust me; they enjoy the game of manipulation a lot.

• You're trusting and vulnerable to everyone. If unlike most people, you naturally trust people and expect them to do the right thing and treat you with respect, then a narcissist will likely use this to their advantage. He or she knows it's easy to get away with lying and deceit because you never doubt their actions or motives. They also see your openness and vulnerability as a weakness to be exploited for personal gain.

Chapter 04: Tools of manipulation

Toxic people like malignant narcissists engage in maladaptive habits that ultimately exploit, hurt, and demean their family members, friends, and intimate relationships. They will usually use a variety of tactics that distort the reality of their victims and are really good at deflecting responsibility. Check to see if you've experienced any of these in the past or present within your relationships. And as soon as you recognize an active tactic in your life, apply the helpful suggestions provided.

1. Gaslighting

It is the most stealthy and manipulative tactic out there. When a narcissist gaslights you two conflicting beliefs battle it out: is this person right or do I trust what I experienced?

A manipulative narcissist will usually throw statements at you like "that didn't happen," "are you crazy?" or "you're imagining things." He or she will try to convince you that you can't trust your own ideas anymore.

Do this:

As soon as you become aware that someone in your life is gaslighting you, ground yourself in your own reality. Journal your thoughts or speak to a close friend so you can find the strength to resist this need to make yourself dysfunctional and the other person right. The more you can validate your own thoughts and reality, the easier it will be to trust your inner guidance rather than ideas coming from a person who always makes you feel wrong.

2. Avoiding accountability at all costs.

Narcissists usually use this tactic when they don't want to own up to something. He or she will literally change the actual topic and redirect attention to a different issue altogether. For example, if you start complaining to your narcissistic husband about their neglectful parenting, he might bring up the one mistake you committed even before the children were born. To spot this in your life, take note of when the person starts deviating from the topic at hand. Usually he or she will say something like "What about that time when you..."

Do this:

The next time someone tries to derail you, give him or her the chance to speak, listen, and gently (but firmly) bring him or her back to what you were saying. Act like a broken record and keep stating the facts without giving in to their tactic. If they are not interested, step back, preserve your energy, and move on to something more constructive.

3. Name-calling

Narcissists generally blow things out of proportion, especially when they feel threatened in any way. Narcissistic rage is very common, and as Mark Goulson, M.D says, narcissistic rage does not result from low self-esteem but rather a very high sense of entitlement and a false sense of superiority. Name-calling is one of the lowest forms of rage demonstrated by narcissists who want to degrade and insult your intelligence or appearance quickly. They also use it to criticize beliefs, opinions, and insights.

Do this:
End all interactions and communication once someone starts name-calling you. Let him, or her know you will not tolerate it and make sure you don't take things personally. Internalizing, it only gives them the joy they were seeking to begin with. Realize there is a hidden deficiency and insecurity that's driving them to act so lowly.

4. Covert and overt threats.

Malignant narcissists usually get very offended and threatened by anything that challenges their sense of entitlement, superiority, and grandiosity. They impose unrealistic demands on those around them, and when those needs aren't meant rather than deal healthily with conflict or try to find a compromise, they will usually resort to threats. Because they are always right and must always win, your perspective or feelings are never taken into consideration. This makes it impossible to ever truly satisfy a narcissist.

Do this:

Whenever someone threatens you in any way for having a different opinion or perspective, take it seriously and see it as a red flag. If you are already dealing with a narcissist that's threatening your well being in any way, start taking action. Document these threats and report them to the appropriate authority; don't wait till it's too late.

5. Projection.

This is another tactic commonly used by malignant narcissists because they are usually unwilling to see their own shortcomings. When dealing with such a person, he or she will do everything in their power to avoid being held accountable for their actions and especially their deficiencies. Projection is a defense mechanism used to deflect one's own negative behavior and attributing it to someone else. According to Narcissistic Personality Disorder clinical expert Dr. Martinez-Lewi, the projections of a narcissist are often psychologically abusive. Instead of acknowledging their own flaws, imperfections, and wrongdoings, malignant narcissists choose to dump their personal traits on their victims in ways that are usually very cruel and painful.

For example, if your partner often calls you "clingy" in an attempt to make you feel like you're the one who is dependent on them, then you're probably being manipulated using this tactic. Malignant narcissists love to shame others and play the blame shifting game. Usually, it's you and/or the world that is to blame for everything that's wrong with them. And your job as their victim is to nurse and babysit that fragile ego.

Do this:

Stop projecting your compassion and empathy on to such people and by all means, stop carrying the burden of their toxicity. Don't own any of their projections. You don't have to live in someone else's cesspool of dysfunction anymore, so cut off those ties and put an end to the blame game.

6. Love-bombing and devaluation.

Malignant narcissists at first seem very charming and attentive. They idealize you until you're hooked and emotionally invested in the relationship then they begin devaluing you. They are notorious for putting their intimate partners up on a pedestal at the start of the relationship and a few months in turn things around drastically. But this isn't the only tactic used. Sometimes the narcissist will put you on a pedestal and devalue their ex. Unfortunately, when the dust settles, you'll be on the same receiving end that same experience because the very thing they admire about you now might become the insults they throw around to devalue you.

Do this:
Be more mindful of how a person speaks or treats other people. Don't get too carried away with receiving over the top attention and praise, especially at the start of a relationship. It might

end up clouding your judgment. Know that the way someone speaks and treats their previous partners is potentially the way you'll be treated in the future.

7. Triangulation.

This is a widespread trick between lovers. Malignant narcissists love to evoke jealousy and uncertainty by playing this card. They will use strangers, co-workers, ex-partners, friends, and even family members if they have to. It's a tactic used to distract you from the unhealthy, abusive behavior he or she may be exposing you to so you can have a false image of them. They want to appear desirable and can go to any lengths to show just how important they are and how "everybody wants to be with them." It usually works well to manufacture love triangles that often hurt the victims and leaves them feeling unhinged.

Do this:

Step back from the triangulation and increase your awareness. Recognize that everyone under the influence of the narcissist is mostly being played and that you are all victims of this sick game. Then decide who you want to be. Seek out your own validation and if necessary, gain support from someone outside the narcissist's circle of influence.

8. Aggressive blows disguised as jokes.

Covert narcissists enjoy taking pleasure at your expense so it shouldn't come as a surprise that humor is used to inject shame, humiliation, and pain into your experience. They are not "just jokes," and you're not paranoid or too stuck up. These people just want to get away with saying appalling things while still preserving their calm demeanor. This is one I have experienced a lot in my old relationship. Each time I would say something, my abuser would claim I have no sense of humor. I realize now that narcissists gain pleasure when we feel hurt. This type of verbal abuse also infuses the gaslighting tactic because if you question or react to an appalling remark, the narcissist usually says, "it's just a joke. Geez. Why are you so sensitive?" which then makes you doubt yourself.

Do this:

Regardless of the situation, learn to stand up for yourself. You don't have to be aggressive or physical about it, just clearly communicate what you can and cannot tolerate. Call out the manipulative narcissist on his or her game and let them know it is not okay. Distance yourself from such people and avoid any further interactions if possible.

9. Control.

Malignant narcissists want to control everything. The conversation, the meals, the social outings, finances - literally everything. But the most important thing they love gaining control over is your emotional state. They love toying with your emotions. Disagreements about trivial things, rage, and conflicts that come from nowhere are all tactics to keep your emotions off balance. They will emotionally withdraw and the re-idealize you once they feel like they're losing you and keep swinging from the false self to the true self to keep you on the emotional edge. Psychologically you can never feel sure about who your partner really is.

The more power a narcissist has over your emotions, the less likely you'll trust in your own reality, whether it's a parental or intimate relationship.

Do this:

Seek out help so you can reclaim your emotional power and take back control in your life. Find your power once more because it's the only way people will cease to control and take advantage of you.

Chapter 05: The science and psychology behind narcissistic relationships

The effects of narcissistic abuse run far deeper than physical harm. In fact, modern science has proven that consistent emotional trauma over a long period can cause victims to develop both PTSD and C-PTSD. There are also detrimental physical effects on the brain when one is suffering from consistent emotional abuse. Medical scientists have found that victims experience a shrinking of the hippocampus and a swelling of the amygdala, both of which carry serious consequences.

Your brain on trauma

The hippocampus: This is the part of your brain responsible for short-term memory. Information is stored in short-term memory before it gets converted to permanent memory.

Without short-term memory, learning becomes very difficult.

In a study from Stanford University and the University of New Orleans, they found there was a strict correlation between high levels of cortisol (a stress-induced hormone) and decreased volume in the hippocampus. The more stressed a person is, the smaller their hippocampus becomes.

The Amygdala: This is the part of our brain responsible for our fight or flight reaction. Also known as the reptilian brain, it controls our primal emotions and functions including fear, hate, lust as well as our breathing and heart rate.

Malignant narcissists usually create an atmosphere for their victims where the amygdala is continually stimulated and continuously on the alert. This is very detrimental to the well-being of the victim and often results in a permanent state of anxiety and fear. Even after the victim survives such a horrid experience they will continue to have PTSD symptoms, increased phobias, panic attacks and so on because their enlarged amygdala is so used to seeking out and experiencing that state of fear.

Unfortunately, the psychological harm and effects of being exposed to narcissistic abuse, whether physical or emotional or both can push your brain activity beyond the zone of effectiveness. A damaged hippocampus can cripple everything you do, learn, and impede your progress. This is because the brain needs to create new neural pathways to learn new things, and that process usually takes place in the hippocampus. But if you're releasing too much cortisol all the time due to the stressful nature of your relationship, the cortisol will attach the neurons in the hippocampus (causing it to shrink) and stimulate the amygdala which in turn affects your thoughts and mental activity so that instead of being focused, productive and happy, you feel stressed, constantly worried and fearful of everything.

Why the emotional and psychological abuse?

Narcissists crave and depend on validation and praise from the external world. When you are a loving, giving sensitive person it's only natural that you'll generously give what the narcissist wants and although at a surface level this doesn't seem like such a bad story, the underlying consequences of a prolonged relationship that's one-sided and solely focused on satiating the monster needs of another are anything but positive. It's almost impossible to create a healthy balanced, nourishing relationship when in a relationship with a narcissist whether they genuinely care about you or not.

We like to believe that loving another means accepting them fully just as they are with flaws and all. That it's not our place to try and make people become what they are not but simply love them as they are. But what this does is create an incredibly negative experience for us where we feel stuck in something detrimental to our well-being and happiness. The psychological abuse becomes inevitable when dealing with a narcissist because you won't always be able to live up to their endless demands and needs. As soon as you don't fit into their plans, their nature is to punish and inflict pain in whatever way possible. Because everything is about them, they will never listen to your needs and will tend to downplay your interests and feelings, which alone becomes the start of an unhealthy relationship. I believe that the main reason behind the pain and suffering narcissists inflict has something to do with their inability to connect and love another human being deeply. A narcissist's heart either hasn't developed or has been shut down due to early psychic trauma such as being raised by narcissistic parents. It is this crippling handicap both emotionally and spiritually that hinders their ability to connect and dims their intuitive guidance, empathic abilities, and love.

Narcissistic supply

This is a concept that was introduced into psychoanalytic theory by Otto Fenichel in 1938. It's typically used in a negative sense to describe the excessive need a malignant narcissist has for attention, praise, and admiration from others. Simply stated, narcissistic supply is energy, and it's what you are feeding your abuser as long as you're active in the relationship. It can be positive energy in the form of compliments, praise and affection or negative energy in the form of arguments, fights, etc.

You give them attention, validate their ideas, and in a weird way, keep their false self alive and powerful. I know they like to call you needy, but the truth is, they need you for their own survival. Narcissists need to suck energy and attention from people to feel alive, and they need a constant distraction to drown out their inner screams of defectiveness and dysfunction. The more they get supplied, the more they want it and will continue to play their mind games until they feel they've had enough then it'll be time to move on to the next supplier.

I see it more like a drug for the narcissist because this "supply" is what provides the emotional life force they need without which they would probably self-destruct. I believe it is the reason behind all their manipulative and abusive actions. When a narcissist spots a potential supplier, which is usually someone vulnerable to narcissistic abuse or other types of trauma, they see that as an open opportunity to get ahead, and you can be sure, they will stop at nothing to get their daily supply.

Now that you understand the narcissist in your life has a false self to recognize that this false self is dependent on gaining validation, praise, and admiration to confirm its existence. This is usually achieved through external means because the narcissist is unable to generate a sense of wholeness from within. As a consequence of paying the ultimate price for the disowned inner self, he or she seeks out external supply in the form of narcissistic victims.

In deeply contemplating why malignant narcissists love to abuse their victims I have come to the conclusion that it is because they need to feel alive and the only way they know how to do it is by putting others down and taking from them the healthy emotional energy they sense from their victim in an attempt to fill the void within. In other words, "supply me with the version of me that is missing, so I can escape the "dead" inner version of myself." Makes sense, doesn't it?

The cycle of abuse

Highly experienced narcissists seduce their prey without ever touching them. They learn your love language quickly and know how to appeal to what you enjoy hearing. Winning your love is a great distraction (to their hidden issues) that they truly enjoy. As they draw you into their trap there's no end to the foreplay both verbal and physical they are willing to do, and in this chivalry, most of us fall head over heels for these charming devils. There seems to be a clear cycle that most narcissists take their victims through. Sometimes I wonder if there's a manual written for them that the rest of us are unaware of. Here's the cycle of doom that usually leaves the narcissist's prey in utter despair.

Idealization and love-bombing:

This phase can best be described as ecstasy for both the narcissist and the victim, especially in intimate relationships. During this phase, the narcissist will give constant attention and affection, excessive praise, flattery, and put us up on a pedestal. For many of us, we blindly fall for this tactic and unknowingly become devoted and times disturbingly close to worshiping them. The words and actions of the narcissist though hollow seem too good to pass up and we begin to invest everything. Malignant narcissists do a great job mirroring our needs and deepest desires; sometimes even our interests and points of view.

Soon enough, the hope of a brighter loving future and your dream relationship starts to feel like the only possible reality, and you get addicted to the showers of affection. If it's an intimate relationship, the romance and lovemaking are heavenly, and you can't get enough of it. It's filled with just the right amount of tenderness and aggression, and the narcissist really knows how to bring you to greater heights. Bonding takes place, and you assume the feeling is genuine and mutual. It feels like you just met your soul mate; your twin flame; the one you were made for.

The connection is so heightened during this love-bombing phase it causes you to invest your spiritual, emotional, physical and even biological attention and before too long you're relying on this new fantastic person for survival, and that's when trouble begins.

During this idealization phase, the cracks within the mask that the narcissist is wearing start to show, but most people are too smitten to notice the signs. Those who are lucky and super mindful might pick up on it and recognize the empty shell beneath all the charm and quickly exit the fatal relationship, but this is still rare. For more of us, even if the false masks slip occasionally and we get a sneak peek of the true self of the narcissist, we don't realize what's happening until things are deep and dark.

Devaluation:

This phase usually begins with a shift that you can "feel" but not easily articulate. You're not sure why or how but something changes. He or she cuts down communication and becomes withdrawn and moody. With other people, they seem to be acting the same, but with you, something is definitely off. The playful, flirtatious nature and praises that used to be yours now pass over and land on the ears of others. Instead of the endless affection and attention, you start getting criticism, harsh insults, and sudden inexplicable outbursts. When he or she pulls away, it's with great force and lack of concern, and you start to see how much they enjoy humiliating you. They enjoy provoking you, making you jealous and bringing in others into the dynamic of your relationship, whether that's an ex, a friend, etc. Then there's the stone-cold silence after stonewalling you during arguments. You literally feel that invisible solid wall placed between you two as they go into full mode silent treatment. I find it to be an inexplicable sense of being trapped yet tethered as you ache for the person you first met.

Being devalued makes you feel like you're worthless. The verbal and emotional battery inflicted by a narcissistic abuser shreds your self-esteem and saturates your mind with disempowering belief systems and messages of unworthiness.

Living feels like a battle that never ends.

The Discard:

Even if you find a way to escape a relationship with a malignant narcissist the problem doesn't end there because most of them tend to stalk and harass their victims even years later especially if you're dealing with a vindictive type.

For the victims that don't find a way to escape before it's too late, a horrific trauma is what awaits them once the narcissist chooses to dispose of them. After having your mind, body, and soul violated used and destroyed by someone you believed to be a perfect soul mate, you are then subjected to the ultimate betrayal that hinders you from having closure in the relationship.

This discard phase is often very painful humiliating and unforgettable for the victim. In such cases, one is left feeling depleted, drained, belittled, diminished, and with more questions than answers; more doubt than certainty. It's no wonder so many victims of narcissistic abuse fall into depression and suffer symptoms of trauma. In some cases, victims have even committed suicide because they just couldn't deal with reality after such an ordeal.

Unfortunately, most people are not familiar with the cycle of abuse, and they have very little understanding of what the abuser's world is like. This means that for the most part, after facing such a traumatic experience, the victim will tend to blame himself or herself for being abused. But as you read this, I want to assure you, this is far from the whole truth. A narcissistic abuser or any type of abuser would continue to hurt and harm people whether you were around or not. Their unresolved wounds and issues are not your fault.

In 1979 Leonor Walker made an illustration that is very useful in helping us understand how we got stuck in an abusive relationship and why it's so hard to get out.

Tension building: This is where the abuser turns into a grumpy frowning person always finding any reason to poison the air around you. They become pissed at everything, nothing you do seems right, and they have this glare in their eyes.

The incident: This is where the malignant narcissist has an outburst. Narcissistic rage is the common term, and for most of them, name-calling and other verbal abuse are used. Some even go to the extreme of physical abuse at this point. For example, I once worked with a client who was healing from an extremely narcissistic father. It had taken him years to forgive and mend the broken relationships in their family, and one time, he shared with me some stories of when his dad would have "rage episodes." He would go from sheep to wolf in an instant, and although he never physically laid hands on him or his mom, the guy would punch the wall or smash the windscreen of his car in a total rage.

The reconciliation: For the malignant narcissist, reconciliation just means being able to justify their outburst and rage. It is usually a combination of blaming it on something or someone else and playing the victim.

The calm phase: This phase happens when the narcissist gets distracted and temporarily gets consumed by a new interest. This can be a new relationship, a promotion at work, traveling, or some other self-serving experience. If you happen to be the reason for their distraction, then you'll be encountering the narcissist at their very best, which means you may not quickly detect that you are dealing with a narcissist. But what exactly are you distracting them from?

Their own anger. Malignant narcissists and all types of abusers are outraged people, and they lash out at other people because they don't know how to handle with their inner turmoil.

When you first interact with a malignant narcissist whether it's an adult to an adult relationship or if you were born to a narcissistic parent, things were great because you were their distraction. It helped him, or her feel good to be distracted by you but over time as life happens cracks start showing up, and you (the distraction) stopped being enough for them to suppress all the anger that was bubbling underneath. All of a sudden, he or she becomes a different person. You start to experience some tension building even though you don't know why, they become irritable, edgy, and the same things they used to praise about you become unbearable to them.

And of course, the cycle begins for them in your presence. It never crosses your mind that the person may just be an angry narcissist; instead, you try your best to come to their rescue to get things back into that calm phase.

Having read this far, I can assure you, the best and only path left after such an ordeal is the long road to healing and reclaiming personal power. If you are tired of being entangled in the games of a narcissist and you want to make sure it never happens to you or someone you care about, healing yourself is the only way forward. You must make sure to take necessary measures so that you don't get sucked back into that pit of drama, despair, and abuse.

Chapter 06: Narcissism at work and in relationships

Narcissistic relationships, whether with parents, loves, or colleagues, can make life utterly miserable. People suffering from any type of disorder but especially malignant narcissism carry tremendous pain deep within but they pretend it's not there and instead prefer to lash out and punish other people just to ease their pain. They are not willing to deal with the pain and anger in their lives, so they are constantly battling it out in very unhealthy ways that harm people around them. One of the main coping mechanisms they use is to mute out their empathy or compassion for other people. They learned not to show emotions or get vulnerable with anyone, which hinders their ability to connect and care for another human being genuinely. If you have been raised by a narcissist or currently feel stuck in a narcissistic relationship either at work or in your private life, I want to help you find a way out and be free mentally, emotionally, physically and spiritually.

Narcissistic parents

Being the child of a narcissist is tough. You exist to make your parent look good and to serve their endless demands. Children of narcissists endure years of psychological anguish before reaching the painstaking realization that something is very wrong. Of course, not all children grow up to make this connection, and so chances of healing from it are minimal. Clinical psychologist Dr. Seth Meyers said, "The reality of narcissistic parenting couldn't be sadder. The child of the narcissist realizes early on that he exists to provide a reflection for the parent and to serve the parent- not the other way around. The problem with being a child of a narcissist is that it takes these children so many years of frustration and anguish to figure out that mom or dad isn't quite right. Until that point, these children are merely dancing as fast as they can, trying to please the impossible-to-please narcissist parent. It takes years to finally see that the type of parenting they've been receiving is wrong if not emotionally abusive."

That was my story as a child of a narcissistic dad. And when I finally did a little digging and realized my mom was coming from a long line of victims of narcissistic abuse, I couldn't take it anymore. I decided it needed to end with me before I passed on the same belief systems and tendencies to my future children. There's no doubt about it, growing up as a victim of narcissistic abuse alters the way you grow up and perceive yourself in the world.

A member of my online community who also grew up with a narcissistic parent said that she spent her entire childhood wishing mom would go away and that whenever they were at home, she was always praying someone would come to visit so the insults and mockery would subside for a while. Her mom was incapable of genuinely showing interest or acknowledging anything good in her daughter. Even her most significant accomplishments at school were downplayed. Like many of us, she felt utterly unworthy and undeserving of affection or genuine praise. People treating her with kindness totally freaked her out because her mom had only exposed her to mockery and mistreatment.

How do narcissistic parents see their children?

As long as you are not perceived as a threat by your narcissistic mom or dad and as long as you can make them proud, they'll be okay towards you. They see you as an extension of themselves. Usually, when you're young, there are lesser issues because you haven't yet become an independent thinker. Trouble grows as you get older because the moment you become difficult or can't live up to their expectations then you become an obstacle, a problem they must deal with.

I could go on and on about the trauma of growing up with narcissistic parents but rather than dig deeper into wounds you know all too well, let's focus our attention on how to deal with our parents during our journey of healing.

It's not likely that you can completely eliminate all contact from your parent because even in the case of death, if that wound is still active you will continue to experience their presence in your mind and worse still you may attract more relationships that are similar to that old one. Therefore, it's not a question of running away, but rather, how can you permanently heal and gain freedom? And once you have found your freedom, how do you deal with them when necessary? Here's my solution for this:

• Start by self-reflection to see how your parental relationship influences your behavior. Before you can start the journey of freedom and rewrite your destiny, you need to do the uncomfortable work of looking within to see how badly the narcissist has affected you in your life. Then you must diffuse those aspects so that he or she can have less power over you. Things like fear of disappointing your parent, difficulty expressing your feelings and desires, fearing his or her tantrums and rage episodes are all signs that you were raised by a narcissistic parent. You've probably adapted yourself over the years to cope with these signs, and your parent now understands how to press your buttons. Dr. Alan Rappaport says that co-narcissistic people, as a result of their attempt to get along with their narcissistic parents work hard to please others, defer to other's opinions, worry about how others think and feel about them, are often depressed or anxious, find it hard to know their own views and experience and take the blame for interpersonal problems.

So once you are brave enough to recognize the damage that has been inflicted choose to educate, empower, and heal yourself. I always recommend seeking professional help first because that's what worked for me. The fact that we are dealing with childhood trauma makes it difficult to overcome the entire experience on your own and catching your own blind spots is impossible so best to find a professional that you can trust who is trained to deal with such sensitive matters.

• Recognize that you are dealing with abnormal parental behavior.

Don't just gloss over your situation as stressful. I know as children, we all want to do right by our parents, and usually, we desire to find a mutually beneficial way of fixing our dysfunctional family. But when dealing with a person suffering from a narcissistic personality disorder, the option of mutually beneficial doesn't exist. It's always going to be their way or the high way.

In my family drama, my father demanded that I either do things his way or hit the road and goodness me that was the best decision I ever made in my life. It was the beginning stages of me escaping the trap of his abuse.

• *Refuse to be gaslighted anymore.*

It is a common thing for malignant narcissists to try to convince their children that they are crazy and delusional. If your parent is continually telling you that you're being loony or that your version of events is the wrong one, then it's time you stopped doubting yourself and trust more in your thoughts. This doesn't mean that you'll always recall everything with perfect accuracy but what I want to drive home for you is that your ability to interpret and define what's real to you should be in your power to control. Don't let your reality be dictated by someone who is always looking to be right and have things their way.

• Accept that friends and other family relatives may not understand your situation.

Unless someone has experienced being with a narcissist, it's tough to get him or her to see the hidden abuse you might be undergoing. More often than not, the narcissist is so charming and normal (wearing their mask) in front of other people that it's hard to receive full support or help from them. They'll often say "she'll come around" or "she's the only mother you'll ever have." That's why I encourage you to seek professional help or a community of other survivors and healing victims. Don't feel guilty for taking action to heal and protect yourself even if others don't agree with the extensive measures you take.

• Set firm boundaries.

A malignant narcissist usually has no respect for personal boundaries, so you'll find your parent overstepping reasonable boundaries just to prove they are in control. You are allowed to have your own life and your individual needs and desires. Since a narcissistic parent cannot understand this, establish boundaries that protect your well-being, and make sure you include the necessary consequences of violating said boundaries.

• *Silence that inner critic.*

The learned voice of internal judgment is perhaps the biggest poison that will eat at you if you don't do something about it. And have you noticed that voice sounds just like your parent? In fact, it was likely nurtured by him or her. This is why running away from narcissistic abuse doesn't necessarily give you freedom and peace of mind. That constant reminder that you are not good enough or that you will never be loveable can be profoundly damaging to a child. Children who are raised with this frame of mind usually struggle to see their self-worth or believe in their own potential. Over time this a powerful belief that continues to self as reality. It can take years of ake the sting out of such a belief, and y part is that even if you know it's not true, it can still haunt you.

• *Understand that you may need to cut ties with your parent and move on.*

Many victims of narcissistic abuse feel a sense of responsibility like they have to make things work. I have found this usually doesn't end well. Even if you estrange yourself from your parent, if the guilt of doing it taunts you and you end up going back to fix the broken relationship out of guilt, nothing good will come out of that. Your parent will still continue to manipulate, control, and cause harm to your life.

A friend experienced this when she went back to try to fix her relationship after a six-year estrangement. Six months into the newly formed relationship, it became apparent to her that nothing had changed. Nothing was going to improve because her mother did not see this as a second chance or new beginning. Instead, it was an opportunity to get revenge on the six years they were apart. Because it had been many years of being free from the influence of the narcissistic mother, she quickly caught sight of the manipulation that was taking place and lovingly stepped back, this time for good.

"After six months of earnest effort trying to mend our relationship, I realized we had reached the end of the road. I was hoping to have a healthy mother-daughter relationship, but all she wanted was someone to manipulate, and I'm no longer interested in filling that role. So I said goodbye, this time for good and even though I haven't fully made peace with my mother, I do feel I have closure, and I certainly feel more at peace with the absence of my mother."

Narcissistic partners and how to free yourself How to break up with a narcissist

It's now clear that you're in a relationship with someone who is no good for you and you want out. The relationship is exhausting, confusing and saps life force out of you yet you're still in it why?

Malignant narcissists are professional manipulators and so charming it's hard for us to realize what's going on without a little education. Hopefully, at this point, you've learned enough about narcissists to figure out where you're in a relationship with one. And if you are, it's time to liberate yourself.

1. Don't fall for the manipulation tactics any longer.

Now that you know the manipulation tricks and tools they use try to be more aware when the narcissist attempts to use them to draw you into the narcissistic vortex again. Remember narcissists are really convincing, persuasive, and persistent when they want something. If you feel ready to leave, be decisive, stick to your convictions, and move on to a more positive future where you can expect to receive real love.

2. Focus on the future.

Once you've detached from the narcissist, don't look back. It is imperative to focus all your energy on positive empowering forward momentum and activities that make you feel alive. Work on finding yourself and reclaiming your power not justifying the actions of the narcissist.

3. Detach yourself from the need to fix the narcissist or get all your questions answered.

Again, this is something you need to be super wary of because most victims get stuck in a loop long after the relationship has ended. It may not always be easy, but you must silence that voice that wants to keep digging for answers. Let go of the dead past and keep your word to yourself that you will cut all ties permanently.

4. Be kind to yourself.

As you heal and restore your identity and sense of worth, it is essential you show yourself compassion. Learn to forgive yourself. Be kind to yourself and reinforce the belief that you are worthy of a better, more loving relationship. Self-love and self-compassion is the start of all healing, and your future relationships can only get better if you work on loving yourself.

Narcissism at work

There are specific behavior patterns that you'll learn to recognize when dealing with narcissists at work. These people love to create chaos, they are always looking for praise and validation and want other people to do their tasks for them. They like forming clicks, getting ahead, and are usually unhealthily competitive. They do all these things intentionally, and if you let them get to you, they'll quickly claw their way into your mind and start sucking energy from you.

If you've realized you're dealing with a co-worker, subordinate or a boss who is a narcissist, here are some tips to help you cope and handle them better without harming your own sense of wellbeing.

• Manage your own ego and expectations.

With the clear understanding, you have acquired of how narcissism works and how fragile a narcissist's ego is, it's crucial you set the right expectations for yourself. Manage your need to win or be right and learn to heal yourself so that you don't expect too much from such a person. Don't expect a narcissist to see or agree with your point of view or to be thoughtful. Recognize the situation you are in and act mindfully and accordingly to ensure you come off it with the least amount of blows.

• Don't name-call or label them as a narcissist.
Unless you are a medical professional, it's ethically wrong to label anyone anything. Besides, they won't take it very well and might have the perfect reason to exercise revenge if you threaten their self-image.

• Keep your calm when dealing with the narcissist.
Don't react to their drama and don't engage with them beyond what you have to do to get the task accomplished.

• Be clear about what the role is for each of you and what the expectations are. Whether it's you assigning the task or receiving the assignment, make sure you both have clarity on who is doing what so that everyone knows their responsibilities.

• Don't give them personal information.
They don't care about you or your feelings, so don't express your vulnerability as this will only

harm you in the end. Stay focused on the project at hand, keep conversations short,, and purely focused on completing whatever is on the agenda.

• Keep records and openly track the progress of your working partnership.
To help keep things open and avoid the conflict of responsibility, I recommend you record and track everything involved in your working partnership. If it's a project, you're working on together keep open track of it. If it's a meeting, write it down or record it or do it over emails so that all members concerned have records of what's happening and what needs to happen.

These are just a few tips you can customize to suit your particular situation so that you can learn to co-exist with the narcissist at work. I firmly believe that a narcissist should not adversely impact your career, project, or company. With this knowledge, you now have the power to make sure that person never stands in the way of your success.

Whether you are dealing with a narcissistic parent, spouse, colleague, friend, or lover, know that you are not alone in your experience. There are many helpful articles, books, and people sharing their stories online. Find a support group if you don't feel like taking professional therapy. Do your best to start to educate and empower yourself so you can begin healing and enjoying personal freedom and peace of mind.

Chapter 07: How Past Wounds Make Us Susceptible To Toxic Narcissists

Most victims of narcissistic abuse want to know whether their childhood upbringing had anything to do with the fact that they continue to fall into abusive intimate relationships. Sadly, the short answer is yes.

Those of us who experienced traumatizing childhood experiences have wounds, which could be unconsciously leading us to attract the very things we want to escape. For example, if you grew up in a home where you experienced physical abuse from your dad, you'll likely grow up to be a person that attracts lovers who abuse you too. And if you're not the one being abused, you might develop tendencies of lashing out and physically abusing your partners.

But there is something I want to be very clear about. I am not here to point fingers or play the blame game. Just because you grew up a victim of early childhood trauma doesn't mean you should now spend the rest of your life blaming your parents for your messed up life. Our parents may not have given us an environment that supported healthy childhood experiences, but blaming them will not get us any closer to healing. Both your parents did the best job they knew how with the level of consciousness they had. They were most likely victims of traumatic experiences too, given how prevalent unconscious parenting has been in previous generations.

So is it enough to have read this book or articles on the web to help you escape the horrors of narcissistic abuse permanently? Well, reading this book is a starting point, and it does set you on the path of healing, but real and holistic healing can only come from rectifying the traumatic emotional imprints of our childhood.

Only when this happens can we develop a stable and healthy inner identity, which is no longer susceptible to abuse.

Before you can be able to make the connection with how your past has led you to your present and made you a target for narcissistic abuse, let's lay some essential foundations.

What is trauma?

Trauma is the inability to deal with a specific stressful situation, which in turn causes feelings of overwhelm and powerlessness. It happens when one isn't able to process stressful events, experiences, and circumstances to completion and implement a proper resolution. This unresolved tension turns into stress, gets internalized, and becomes stored as a traumatic memory that eventually begins to develop a life of its own. As you saw in an earlier chapter, this internalized stress negatively affects our brain and nervous system over time. The more repeated this cycle, the greater the damage. Not only does it affect your mind and body, but it also shapes your belief systems and inner identity. These traumatic beliefs become your reality, and you can easily remain a victim to them your entire lifetime. Why? Because they become a self-fulfilling prophecy that keeps you stuck in a loop replaying the same unhealthy traumatic patterns and disappointments over and over again.

Each time a trigger occurs, your brain immediately activates that stored traumatic experience, which affects your thinking, emotions, and body.

Perhaps you've experienced a trigger moment as heaviness in your chest, feeling nauseated, a shock of cold ice through your vein or you may start shaking and sweating abnormally. All kinds of processes start firing up, and there's a natural impulse to want to flee, fight, defend yourself, or even shut down and literally struggle to think, answer, or move.

In short, unresolved stress in your life will become a trauma.

One of the critical mistakes that you can make regarding the regulation, management, and healing of your past trauma is to think that the solution to your problem needs to be something logical.

When you were little and growing up, the things that your emotional center needed in order to develop healthily include but are not limited to caring physical touch, soothing words of kindness and affection and simply being with you both physically and emotionally. If you didn't actually feel loved, important, valued, and seen for you who are then an impairment was bound to happen that would create an unhealing wound. But the plot thickens even more.

According to modern scientific research on epigenetics tells us that the ability to switch on or off specific genes is something that's inherited. And if we've come from ancestors who've suffered trauma, then the parts of our brain that could handle stress effectively might be shut down from birth. Instead, what we might have are over formed hyper arousal centers and amygdalae which means rather than anchoring into our core identity and personal power to deal with stressful situations, we would disconnect from our powerful inner being and seek solutions externally. The more we seek external solutions and validations, the more powerless we'd feel because our quest to control the uncontrollable would fall flat. Eventually, we'd give up, withdraw, and learn to accept the fractures created which would set us on the cycle of continued trauma and bad experiences.

If you didn't grow up with a functioning and developing core identity (which was dependent on our right brain and nervous system health and formation) and if we didn't have a parent consciously stepping in to do that for us until we fully developed this ability to handle stress, then we started carrying trauma after trauma because we weren't able to integrate stresses to completion.

As children, we were impacted by the disappointments, the fights, things that frightened us, feeling unsafe and uncomfortable but the thing that created the most damage for us was the fact that a safe, functional caretaker didn't show up to help us heal and integrate these stressful situations back to calmness and safety. The overwhelm of not being able to deal with our own emotions caused us to disengage and seek other ways to self-medicate our feelings as we grew so that we didn't have to deal with all the unresolved wounds.

Instead of growing up to be a healthy adult who is connected to his or her own body, emotions, and real inner power, many of us are stuck in a never-ending loop of dysfunction.

I grew up believing that no one was there for me; no one supported or even valued me. As a result, I continued to create this self-fulfilling prophecy attracting people who help validate that reality. Then I would say, "see? I'm right. I have no one in this world who truly loves me for who I am."

Can you relate?

Well, I can assure you, this disempowered reality all happens when we are not yet healed from past wounds. Until we learn to be anchored into our inner core truth and values in our body, it won't be easy to experience being safe and authentically yourself. When we resolve our core trauma through our nervous system the cells in our body, our right brain and our entire being will experience the permanent shift in reality because the old self-defeating belief systems will be deemed obsolete.

Post-traumatic stress disorder is usually the consequence of not healing and continually piling up more traumas while stuck in that imprisoned state. The constant reoccurring unsafe feeling that is all too familiar to victims of trauma isn't just something made up. It's because you're not yet at home within yourself. I used to suffer greatly for many years, and I promise you, it can be healed. I no longer have any of it, and it's only because I went within myself and worked on healing that invisible aspect of me.

You need to reclaim your real power and reconnect yourself body, mind, and soul. It's the only way to get back your compass of life so you can find your true north and discern things, people, and relationships that are healthy and those that aren't.

People who are manipulative and pathological such as malignant narcissists will jump at the chance to toss us around mercilessly. They will pretend to be what we need then use the fact that we are disconnected from ourselves to their advantage so they can profit from our energy, life force, and resources.

As you are starting to awaken now, I urge you to stop trying to monitor and control people, your thoughts, situations, or any other uncontrollable thing outside of you. I also want you to put an end to the false beliefs that were activated during your childhood because all they do is bring pain and more suffering as you go through life.

The only permanent and best way to end the victim lifestyle and abuse that you've had to endure is to awaken and turn inward to do the necessary work essential to your healing. You need to repair and restore yourself where it matters, and that is at your core being.

At this point in the book, healing and taking action on your road to wellness is all that matters. Before I share the six stages of your recovery, I want to end this chapter with a few red flags that malignant narcissists often use to get into your mind. They use these to trigger your unresolved unconscious reactions so you can forever remain a victim at their mercy. Until now, of course.

Five ways Abusive narcissists get to you

Malignant narcissists are like parasitic worms in that they don't want to completely destroy you because they actually need you (and others like you) to survive and get their daily supply, but at the same time, they bring much harm to their host. If you go a long time unknowingly allowing such a parasite to inhabit your body, the consequences might be grievous. Still, many of us have a hard time permanently moving on and healing even when we realize we're not in a healthy relationship.

A friend told me of a time when she used to date this local celebrity DJ who is well known in our city. A few months after they started dating, he slapped her hard on the face for supposedly asking too many questions in a demeaning tone. To be fair, they were both pretty drunk, and it was one of those Friday nights where lots had happened, so she thought nothing of it. Next day, despite the red flag and a swollen right cheek, she decided to let go of the matter, assuming she had overreacted after too many Gin and Tonics. Several weeks went by, and all seemed heavenly again. The guy was so apologetic and wanted to do everything possible to make it up to her, which he did for a while. Then the violent acts of aggression happened again, and again, and again. But each time an episode occurred, the details were so blurry for my friend, she was always left wondering if the entire thing wasn't her fault. Like a parasitic worm, he was harming her and yet she struggled to put an end to things or even acknowledge that something was wrong with him. It was as though she got slowly numbed out over time and became unable to recognize the web of abuse she was living in. The guy was draining life force and self-esteem out of her. He planted the seed of self-doubt and half the time she struggled to believe in her own thoughts. This went on for a long time with bouts of aggressive fighting increasing until one night the outburst was so massive, she ended up in an emergency room at 4 am with a bleeding nose and a black eye. Her parents quickly intervened, forced her to spend some months in recovery with her grandma in a different state, and so began her healing process.

One can only imagine what horrors would have taken place had she continued dating that man. As charming and romantic as he was, her life was in a lot of danger. The biggest obstacle standing in her way of ending things was the fact that she always felt like it was her fault.

This is something many of us experience, and I am convinced it's because malignant narcissists do such a great job getting into our heads. They know how to corrupt and brainwash us into thinking we are the ones doing something wrong.

If you still have an active parasite in your head then whether you've physically left that abusive relationship or not, your healing cannot actually take place. Backsliding and getting sucked into the web of abuse will be all too easy. That's because your abuser still knows how to press all the right buttons to make you succumb. Here are a few tricks you want to become aware of as you start your journey to wellness.

• Malignant narcissists are great at making you think - you are the problem.

As mentioned during the section on manipulation tactics, gaslighting is something many abusers use to control their victims. Your abuser might be convincing you that your perception of the abuse is "all in your head."

You may also get remarks like "you like to provoke me" or "you're too sensitive." This is especially true after a rage episode. He or she will try to plant a seed of doubt and remark upon your emotional instability "your issues" to displace blame of his or her abuse as your fault.

• You're my everything; I can't live without you. This is something many of us have heard, and it usually works because rather than terminating that relationship for good we find a way to create a repeat cycle of the same abuse that ends in our anguish. How many of us have fallen for this lie over and over? We keep hoping it's going to get better but rarely does it ever get better.

• Malignant narcissists like to say; " I knew I would regret having you in my life."
What this does is it psychologically mess with your innate desire to feel good enough. As crazy as this may sound when your abuser says this to you, it makes you want to cling on to the relationship even more. You'll feel like you must actively stay in that relationship and prove him or her wrong. For example, if you're in an intimate relationship with a narcissist and they say this to you, then you won't want to leave that

person because you want to show them how wrong they are and how good you can be. This might cause you to compromise yourself, suppress your ideas, opinions and even let them do ridiculous things such as spend all your money just because you want to show them that you are better than what they claim.

• They will use smear campaigns to press your buttons.

This is where your abuser does everything possible to make it seem as though you're the one who is unstable and causing harm. Smear campaigns get in your head and accomplish three main things. First, you become the abuser or unstable person in your relationship. Second, it triggers and provokes you thus proving your instability to others and lastly, it serves as a hovering technique in which the malignant narcissist tries to suck you back into the traumatic relationship.

• Let's just be friends.

This just means the narcissist wants to keep you in their circle of supply so that whenever they need you, they can just pick you up, use you and discard you as and when necessary. Please don't fall for this one because it's one that really gets to many of us even after we are made aware. Your caring nature and the need to forgive and love everyone should not include actively maintaining a friendship with a malignant narcissist.

" Healing does not mean the damage never existed. It means the damage no longer controls our lives."

Chapter 08: Healing Trauma and permanently detaching

Have you just left or are you currently thinking of leaving an abusive relationship behind but you're just not sure of how to completely let go? Do you find yourself thinking about that person, worrying about them and even feeling like you're missing them even when you don't want to?

Are you asking yourself questions like "Why is taking so long to feel free and healed from this situation?" or "Why do I still love this persona after all they've done to me?" or "Will this pain ever go away?"

A lot of people tell me that even after leaving the relationship they still feel like checking the narcissist's social media updates every hour or they keep feeling like sending a text message to see how they are doing or give them a call to get closure on the relationship. These are all urges that naturally come when you start the journey to freedom, and you must learn to resist them.

Obsessing over an emotionally abusive relationship is usually very detrimental to your well-being and causes many to lose their homes, jobs, and even their children. Some people even go as far as attempting suicide and often succeed at it.

I find that most victims and survivors of narcissistic abuse struggle with this aspect of their healing due to one major reason. Namely, they don't learn and practice the art of detachment. It's not always easy, but it's so important you do it when recovering from narcissistic abuse.

What is detachment?

Detachment is a deliberate choice that you make when you're trying to pull yourself away from a toxic relationship. It's a deliberate and conscious decision to no longer be in partnership with the toxic person. But it's important to know that it doesn't just happen all at once. Just because you choose to detach from your narcissistic spouse, for example, doesn't mean it all happens in an instant. It's a starting point, but it will take time, and that's okay especially because frequently there are other complications involved such as children, relatives or business obligations to take care of before one can completely cut out their abuser. In some cases, it's not even possible to cut someone out wholly (which makes detachment even more useful).

Detachment starts to have a positive impact when you consciously refuse to get sucked into the web of lies and manipulative games that a narcissist likes to play. You have to decide that you will no longer accept being demeaned and that you will stand up for yourself when he or she disrespects or belittles you. Because trauma bonding is so addictive, when you do start detaching from your narcissist, it will feel emotionally impossible, and that's why one of the first things you need to do is summon your willpower and cognitive thinking to help you execute. At the start of this, your willpower is what you need to override the emotional patterns, and yes, it will require some effort, but eventually, your emotions will renew and develop their own resilience so that nothing gets to you. But when starting out, focus on the facts and your willpower to avoid getting sucked back into the abuse.

Change begins with you.

If you genuinely want to transform, heal, and rebuild your life after experiencing narcissistic abuse, you have to be willing to change your mind and let go. It all depends on and begins with your intense desire for change and freedom. The more you educate yourself on what a narcissist is and make a conscious effort to strengthen yourself mentally, emotionally, spiritually, and physically, the easier the recovery will be. With awareness comes more possibility and power. You can be able to spot when you're getting sucked into yet another unhealthy relationship or when someone is playing mind games with you. It's also easier to catch yourself repeating old patterns of thought before things get too far. The more empowered you feel, and the more you choose to work on your core healing, the more permanent your new life will be.

If you find yourself always talking about the narcissist and reliving the experiences at every opportunity you get, then you're certainly falling off the path of recovery. If you're still unable to resist the urge to call, text, or stalk them on social media, then for sure, you need help detaching and healing.

Here's what I mean:

Gloria was repeatedly sharing her story over and over again about the state of her traumatizing marriage.

"I realized my husband had NPD years ago and our couples therapist said he had it and referred him to psychotherapy. He has been in therapy, and we are on our 6th psychologist in 8 years. This therapy seemed to help especially EFT but only during the session, and maybe the day after then, he would bounce back. At first, when I started seeing the changes, I finally had hope again. However, he destroys my hope over and over again when he relapses into his old self. He's mean, angry, disrespectful, and rude and has no compassion. In fact, this list could go on and on, but I don't want to dump everything on you guys. I'm done! I've stayed because we have a son. I've left him twice and came back. Now, I know I will walk away and not come back, but I'm afraid of him. His stepson says he is evil. His own 6 years old son says he's a demon. I'm scared of what he will do to my boys or me. I've felt trapped for 8 years. He's in the military, navy seal and due to their "brotherhood," I'm afraid his unit and the public will help only him. But I can't stay. Oh and he says he has PTSD which I totally thought was true, but now I just think he's an a*****e. The good news is I'm onto him. The bad news is he knows I'm weak. Help please!"

Clearly, Gloria is in pain and desperately needs to detach and heal from this trauma before it permanently destroys her. Unfortunately, she is stuck in that same pattern sharing that same story in our community and across social media. Even when she does walk away, it's not long till she finds herself back in the same spot. She is a perfect example of the self-fuelling prophecy that we put lock ourselves in when we don't consciously choose to take responsibility and work on true detachment and healing. Permanently healing from trauma isn't something that can happen by merely venting in a forum or reading a few articles on the topic. It's usually something that requires a great deal of effort, support, professional help, and a strong mindset. Check in with yourself to see where you stand relative to your particular situation. Have you really gotten to the point where you've made a real, deliberate, and conscious decision to make a change?

Have you truly decided to take back your power and heal your identity regardless of how powerful the narcissist has been in your life? Are you willing to change your mind, develop your will power and resist those old urges and triggers that usually keep you stuck? If you answered yes to all the questions, here are six steps I invite you to employ as you start your journey to healing and transformation.

The six steps of your recovery

There are many elements involved during the healing process, and just as with any loss and recovery program, there will be periods of grieving, denial, anger, and even depression. The main difference between a typical breakup and narcissistic abuse recovery, the natural phase of acceptance doesn't naturally follow.

Victims of narcissistic abuse usually remain fixated and even obsessed about their abuser, often suffering for decades post-breakup. Some of the stories I have shared with you in this book already alluded to this reality. This partial healing, in turn, keeps them in that repetitive pattern of doom where the only other relationships that can come to fruition during that unhealed phase will be more of the same or similar to the heartache, pain, and abuse they were once subjected to. Needless to say, this is not true healing and certainly doesn't offer the life of freedom and love that I want every survivor to experience after facing narcissistic abuse.

To make sure you completely heal and from your abusive relationship and never again drain your energy obsessing over someone who doesn't deserve your affection, try the following steps.

Step One: Learn grounding techniques and self-soothing methods.

Narcissistic abuse is an emotional trauma that targets your primal abandonment wound as we learned earlier. When you experience betrayal, rejection, and neglect by the narcissist, your amygdala hijacks your rational thinking and triggers your fight, flight, or freeze mode.

For example, the next time you have the thought "I've been rejected because I'm not good enough," a painful emotion will be triggered from that thought that is most likely sadness, depression, panic, etc. The natural instinct that tends to kick in when this happens is to accept and sprint with said emotions like a Running Back on crack with blinders on. I need you to stop in those heated moments and instead create a buffer period that enables you to practice self-soothing methods and grounding techniques that will dampen that emotional hijacking.

While it may not be possible to completely prevent those moments from happening (at least not in the beginning), it is possible to ease your way out of it as soon as you catch yourself getting hijacked. Self-soothing is the most critical step to learn once you start your journey to healing and must be practiced even if you're still in the abusive relationship. The more you can gain power over your emotions and create buffer periods that allow you to breathe, ground yourself, and take charge of your mind, the easier it will be overcome the abusive relationship. Without proper and effective grounding and soothing techniques, any activities you engage in will not yield positive results because your brain will always be hijacked by your wounded amygdala. There are many excellent grounding techniques that you can find online, but here are just a few that many professional therapists advice.

1. Cross your arms, rock, and breathe deeply. Crossing your arms gives you a sense of being contained and supported. Rocking mimics the feeling of being a fetus nestled in the womb, safe from the world. Pair this with slow and deep breathing until you feel powerfully soothed.

2. Gentle hand technique. As soon as you feel yourself getting hijacked by your emotions, close your eyes, and focus on your body. Figure out the part of your body that is experiencing this fear the most. Rest a gentle hand over that part of your body (like a mother would over her little one). This is a form of self-parenting which really helps soothe your inner child. Place your hand there with the intention of pouring unconditional love and light on yourself until you feel the fear dissipating.

3. Say a safety statement to yourself. For example, "My name is [fill in the blank]; I am safe right now. I am in the present, not the past. What I am feeling right now is valid, but I don't need it. I can release and put it away. I am safe

right now." If you cannot speak your statement aloud to yourself, then write it down as many times as needed until you feel the shift.

For more grounding and soothing techniques, check out the resources provided at the end of this book.

Step Two: Allow yourself to be angry and grieve.

Just because the relationship with your abuser was one-sided and established on lies doesn't mean you shouldn't allow yourself to grieve, get angry, and experience the pain of it all. The relationship was real for you, regardless of how dysfunctional it was. Not allowing yourself to process these feelings often leads to damaging consequences further down the line. You might end up stuck in an emotional or spiritual rut of bereavement or carry some of that baggage with you to the next relationship. Whenever we don't process and embrace those feelings of anger and grieve, there are usually manifestations that include:

• Feeling emotionless or depressed and sad for prolonged periods of time.

• Prolonged exhaustion, constant fatigue, anxiety, and indifference.

• Falling into one or more addictions as a form of soothing oneself.

• Chronic pain or illness.

• Repeated avoidances.

•Eating disorders and obesity.

• Suppressed anger.

Complicated grief is a serve and long-lasting form of grief that takes over one's life, and unfortunately, it's widespread in the aftermath of an abusive relationship. It is especially true for victims of narcissistic abuse who usually don't get the closure or validation they deserve. That "unfinished business" including unsettled disputes, the discrediting of your character, unanswered questions and unrequited love can leave you hanging and unable to experience completion. Similar to the story I shared earlier of the woman who was left hanging right after getting engaged, that type of experience can leave you feeling stuck in the pain of your grief. This type of grieving is made excruciating by the fact that you have to grieve twice. First for the person who love-bombed you and for whom you fought to bring back amidst soul-shattering abuse and second, you grieve for the end of the relationship.

If you believe you're suffering from any psychological neurosis or complicated grief, then I urge you to seek professional help from a therapist who specializes in abuse and trauma before it's too late. Sometimes you might even have to go on prescribed medication but make sure to inquire about non-addictive types that you can use on those unbearable days. Complicated grief used to be associated strictly with bereavement, but medical professionals now agree that it can apply to any kind of traumatic loss, so please reach out for help if you need it.

Step Three: Stop researching obsessively on narcissism.

I know many bloggers, vloggers, and speakers on this topic will keep saying you need to educate yourself as much as possible and talk about your suffering on as many platforms, chat rooms, and forums as you can, but here's the thing: If you're wanting to transform, heal and restart your life, digging into the old wounds only keeps that reality alive and active.

This isn't to say you should be ignorant. During the awakening and discovery phase, you absolutely need to gain understanding about narcissism, why your partner or parent behaves as they do, what traits make them identifiable, and so on. It's essential in helping you recognize the dynamics of your abusive relationship. But that is just the first phase. Once you awaken and gain awareness, it's time to shift your focus. When it's truly time to heal yourself, you should then place all your attention on the actual healing and the actions you can take. Self-care, self-love, accessing your inner power, reclaiming your identity, processing traumatic emotions, and other healing methods should be the only thing you care about.

Continuing to research on the traits of your narcissistic parent or disordered ex keeps your focus on them, not your healing and recovery. Dr. Dan Siegel, a neuroscientist, often likes to remind us that what fires together, wires together. That's how our brain creates new neural pathways. Each time we repeat a particular thought or action, we are in essence reinforcing the connection between our neurons, which in turn keeps those thoughts active and sees that as the lifestyle we want more of. This is how our day-to-day reality is shaped.

I know this will be difficult to fully implement in the early stages because you'll be rewriting your old thought patterns and beliefs. Shifting from making your abuser the center of your world to making yourself the center of your world is actually easier said than done. But I want you to take it a day at a time and put as much effort as is necessary. Use your willpower to put an end to devoting your attention on the narcissist and train your mind to focus on improving your own life.

Step Four: Develop your self-esteem.

At this point, you want to come to the realization that regardless of the torment, degradation, and rejection, the narcissist put you through; who you are is a powerful being. The perceived identity that was broken by your abuser isn't who you are; you are far more than that. No one can ever really hurt or define your real identity, expect you.

The primary goal of a malignant narcissist is to make you feel invalidated, invisible, and unworthy. So even if the narcissist does actually love being around you and think the world of you, they would never admit it unless they want to take advantage of it in some way. The more you can believe that you're not worthy of love and that you're "damaged goods," the more a narcissist will easily keep you around. They've learned that by destroying your self-esteem and making you feel useless, keeping you around becomes easy.

Step Five: Incorporate movement into your daily routine.

Whether you resonate with Yoga, running, dancing, or other forms of physical activity, releasing endorphins is a crucial step in this healing process. It will help you feel safe and stable and generate the positive feelings that have been torn down from emotional trauma.

I know when in the midst of the pain and suffering, it can be hard to believe that one day you'll experience happiness and love again but trust me, the heart does heal. You just need to foster an environment conducive for healing and physically engaging your body helps create such an atmosphere. Love yourself enough to believe that you deserve refuge from pain, abuse, and suffering.

Step Six: Work on reconnecting with your passion and purpose in life.

Frequently the path to complete healing is impeded by the past and repeated cycles of backsliding. I firmly believe that if you choose to focus on your future and invest your time, energy, and resources going after something that brings you deep meaning and satisfaction, things will fall into place much faster. Even the cravings of your abuser won't have such a significant hold on you because you can quickly refocus on the new idea or project that makes you come alive. Find something that brings you joy and makes you feel like you are making a difference in the world. Something that is bigger than you and even feels impossible to attain at this point in time. Keep your eye on that as you go through the journey of healing and sooner rather than later, you'll discover the old life has fallen off, and your new life is taking shape.

This takes time, practice, determination, and a clear plan. It also requires a lot of self-love, self-care, and the desire to make something good out of your life. Speaking of which, if you're not sure where to start when it comes to practicing self-love and self-care, try some of the tips I am sharing next.

Five self-care suggestions that are integral to your complete healing and transformation

Self-compassion and self-care are integral cornerstones of healing from an abusive relationship. It is often easier said than done because for many of us, learning to love ourselves and see ourselves as special, is one of the most challenging tasks we face.

When you've spent your whole life in a dark place, feeling invisible and worthless, it can be tough replacing that image of yourself with feelings of adoration and love, but that is precisely what you must do to heal and transform your life fully. You must give yourself the gift of love, affection, and adoration because ironically, being able to attract true love and being able to love others well depends on your ability to love yourself. You must retrain your mind to give yourself the very things your narcissistic abuser has tried to take away from you. By practicing self-care and extending love toward yourself, you begin to cultivate feelings of self-worth, strength, and resilience, which is precisely what you need to overcome trauma and narcissistic abuse.

Loving yourself is not selfish or self-centered. I hope you know that. Pointing your compassion inwards fosters increased empathy for those around you and enables you to heal those deeply hidden wounds from your past. When I speak of self-care, I mean every aspect of your being. You need to design for yourself a balanced lifestyle to aid you on this journey of recovery, and that includes exercise, proper nutrition, getting enough sleep, etc. It's also about exerting healthy boundaries for yourself and others, especially the narcissists in your life that you can't completely avoid either due to family or legally binding obligations.

Self-care is also about developing a mindfulness attitude so that you can become more aware of your thoughts, behaviors, and the things that trigger you as well as your behaviors and actions. If you're in resonance with everything I just said, here are some key elements of self-care I encourage you to practice on this journey of recovery and transformation.

1. Physical self-care.

This implies caring for your physical body, both internally and externally. This includes things like

- Getting enough sleep.
- Regularly taking long walks in nature or on the beach.
- Eating healthy, nourishing, wholesome meals.
- Drinking plenty of water.
- Eliminating or reducing beverages that over stimulate your nervous system.
- Exercising and moving your body regularly so you can optimize your energy levels.

2. Emotional self-care.

This is especially important for those of us subjected to trauma and narcissistic abuse. Being able to take back control of our emotions so we can stop being manipulated and emotionally chained to unhealthy situations is paramount to our healing.

You can take care of your emotional well being by processing and verbalizing feelings with trusted friends, a coach, healer, or a professional therapist who specializes in trauma and abuse. You can also release negative emotions through an expressive art form, such as:

• Drawing.
•Painting.
• Listening to music.
• Dancing.
•Singing.
•Playing an instrument.
•Pottery.
• Poetry etc.

One of my closest friends started taking art classes to release the emotional block that had been tormenting her life since childhood. The anger she carried for her narcissistic mother slowly started dissolving when she started even though she wasn't very good at it. Over time, she's not only graduated to an advanced class, but she's also emotionally transformed radiating a happier, lighter and more passionate side that I had never encountered before.

Of course, it also helps that she learned to fully incorporate the technique I will be sharing with you on the next chapter because, at the end of the day, freedom from narcissistic abuse is best enjoyed when one can eliminate situations that cause undue emotional distress. By releasing instead of suppressing your emotions, you can move through painful experiences that may otherwise keep you stuck in permanent suffering.

3. Mental self-care.

Victims and survivors of narcissistic abuse absolutely need this type of self-care. After all, the whole game behind a malignant narcissist is to break you mentally so that you can feel helpless in their power and depend on them. Practice self-care by trying new activities that challenge and stimulate you intellectually. Things like

• Listening to an empowering thought-provoking podcast.

• Completing a puzzle.

• Engaging in deep, inspiring, and meaningful conversation with a friend.

• Immerse yourself in a book that empowers you like Brené Brown's "The Gifts Of Imperfection: Let Go Of Who You Think You're Supposed To Be And Embrace Who You Are."

4. Social self-care.

Although narcissistic abuse makes us more wary of opening up to more relationships, we still need to nurture real relationships with individuals who uplift and support us. Whether it is with a therapist, friend, family member, or community members, create a support system around you and build strong and meaningful relationships. Cut all ties with old relationships that keep you feeling like a victim. A few ways to meet and nurture great social connections could be:

• Volunteering at special events.

• Joining a healing or yoga class.

• Joining a recovery program.

• Joining a mastermind group.

5. *Spiritual Self-care.*

There is no right or wrong way to practice this form of self-care, and each person will need to develop their own ritual based on held beliefs and religious preferences. For some, spirituality is found in the wilderness; for others, it's found in books or retreats. Your spirituality is going to be personal to you and only you. The core thing is to generate feelings of connectedness, oneness, wholeness, and universality. True healing is about coming into your true identity and healing yourself at the very core of your being, and that will require spiritual integration. So figure out what brings you into that space and diminishes loneliness, self-doubt, fear and all other lower states of being. A few practices have been known to bring victims of narcissistic abuse into a place of wholeness. Here are a few suggestions to test out.

• Meditation.

I consider meditation to be one of the easiest and best ways to connect to the spiritual aspect of yourself. Of course, it requires a little effort and commitment, in the beginning, to keep going especially because one generally feels like nothing is happening. When I first started meditating, my thoughts were drowning me, I kept wondering if I was doing it right, and I was doing it with the aim of "making something happen." Here's the thing with meditation - it's not about making something happen; it's about just being with yourself in the present moment and simply basking in your own awareness. So I encourage you to start slowly, for a few minutes each day and soon enough you'll notice many changes taking place within and eventually on the outside as well. I assure you, the benefits of meditation are life changing, including, rewiring your brain's neural activity, reducing stress and giving you more clarity. Once you get the hang of it, you won't be able to imagine life without some daily mediation.

• Yoga.

The intention behind yoga is to harmonize your body, mind, and spirit, and it's usually individualized according to what your needs are at the time. Most people recognize yoga as a form of workout, which is good because indeed it has physical health benefits, but there's more to it than this. For recovering victims and survivors, yoga is especially wonderful at helping us connect with our body and emotions stored deep within.

I encourage you to give it a try for a couple of weeks. It will help you practice non-judgment and self-acceptance with your current situation, which is one of the most challenging things to do when starting your journey of healing. It will also instill a feeling of hope and strength to keep moving forward no matter how bad things are in the moment because you'll know you're slowly building a strong foundation for a more empowering life.

• Spending time in solitude in nature.
Being in nature, heals. The warmth of the sun on your skin, the smell of the earth, sound of birds or water, wind swaying the trees are all great for making your senses come alive and reconnecting you with the flow of life. When in nature, you're in the moment, and there is a sense of experiencing something greater than yourself, which exactly what you need to develop the power and strength to terminate your abusive relationship. As often as you possibly can, take time to be in nature, even if it's just five minutes sitting by a tree in the park.

• Practice Forgiveness.
This is a spiritual practice and trust me, it is easier said than done. When we are the ones being wronged, taken advantage of and abused,

practicing forgiveness can be very challenging. But here's the thing, lack of practicing forgiveness only holds you back from experiencing life and keeps you stuck in the very situation you want to escape.

When we hold on to anger, resentment, or a grudge, we waste a lot of energy that could just as well be directed toward creating a life you love. Remaining in the present moment and accepting both pleasure and pain as part of your journey as a human being will enable you to heal and bring back spiritual health and balance sufficiently. The human ego naturally leans toward pleasure and comfort, but if you really want to get at the heart of who you really are, you need to make an effort and discipline yourself more so you can explore all that you are. The real you isn't afraid, or hurt or damaged by pain, and it is this aspect of yourself that you need to reconnect with to overcome the abuse you've faced. When you practice forgiveness (I mean real forgiveness), you open the door and create the space for the real you to emerge. As I said, this won't come easy, and like all practices, it will take time and effort, but you can do it.

This list is far from conclusive, but you have enough here to start practicing and enjoying the benefits of self-care. Start by testing out one or two things from the examples provided. Keep things simple and focus on doing the ones that feel good to you. If what you try doesn't seem to impact you in any way, try something else. The journey of healing after narcissistic abuse is as much a sacred and spiritual journey as it is physical. There is no right or wrong path. The most important thing is that you work on your inner world, find your true self, live from that space, and implement a self-care plan that makes you feel good throughout this process.

Building your immunity and Identity after narcissistic abuse

Many victims and survivors of narcissistic abuse who've grown up under the web of malignant narcissism hardly know that they are suffering from a loss of self-identity. I can recall when it first dawned on me. It was during one of my first internship interviews where I was faced with a situation and couldn't for the life of me figure out what to do because I didn't even know what makes me different. My interviewer asked me what I think makes me different, and I froze. Reflecting on that moment, later on, I realized that I had no sense of identity or value. I honestly didn't think there was anything special about me. Perhaps you've had similar moments in your life?

If so, then you probably feel a lot of resentment and anger (rightfully so), but I am here to encourage you to find a way to let go and move on. It won't happen all at once, but you can heal and rebuild your immunity and self-identity.

The fact that malignant narcissists work on destroying their victim's self-esteem and identity actually proves that they, too, are dealing with their own identity issues. In many cases, your abuser doesn't know who they really are. They have an ideal they are trying to reach, but since they don't know how to do it in a healthy way, they focus on using you and your resources to do it. Similar to how people with substance abuse issues chase after drugs, alcohol, or gambling for that "high," your abuser chases after attention and energy to get their high.

When it comes to reversing the damage and restoring yourself back into full power, understand that it will take time. It is an ongoing process. Just as it didn't happen overnight, healing your self-image and restoring a healthy inner child won't take place at the snap of a finger. But here are a few things to incorporate throughout your recovery to fast track the process.

• Cultivate self-love.

This isn't just about feeling good or taking time for yourself, it's about cultivating a state of appreciation for yourself. Let's face it, we struggle with feeling self-appreciation a lot. Self-love allows you to embrace and even love your weakness along with your strength. It's about having compassion for yourself as you strive to find personal meaning and fulfillment. Ever heard of a concept called Wabi Sabi? Arielle Ford wrote a book called Wabi Sabi Love that extrapolates the ancient Japanese philosophy of Wabi Sabi, which is the acceptance and affectionate regard for imperfection. This is a principle you must practice on yourself until you get tot he point where all you see and feel about yourself is pure unconditional and perfect love.

• Create a strong support structure around your healing.

Part of rebuilding yourself and fully healing is creating boundaries so that others can know how far they can go with you. Where you choose to draw the line between a healthy relationship and a loss of self-identity will determine how your future relationships shape up. If you don't want a repeat of your past, you need to change within and without. Discern between constructive advice and abusive criticism.

• Go after a dream or desire that the narcissist made you believe you can't accomplish.
This could be a lifelong dream that you've always want to turn into reality, a hobby, a career you wanted to pursue or something you've always wanted to experience. Going after the thing your abuser said you couldn't do is a great way to prove to yourself how wrong they are about you, who you are, and what your potential is. Choose to do stuff that makes you come alive and reconnect you with your inner child.

• Take your time and be easy with yourself during this process. No one expects you to figure it all out. At first, it might be tough to even communicate with other people or trust in your own thoughts. It's okay not to know everything about yourself, how things will turn out, or what your future life will look like. This is all part of healing and regaining your real identity. You won't have all the answers, and some days may still be tough to get through. If you put too much pressure on yourself, move too fast, or force things to be what they aren't yet, you risk ending up in another abusive or toxic relationship.

Take your time to heal, recover, and restore your life on your own terms. It may take a few months or a few years. The important thing is that you build a life you love of true freedom.

Chapter 09: No contact

The troubling thought in today's information-driven world is that the Internet contains a lot of stuff that doesn't really get you anywhere.

You've been there, haven't you?

Looking to end the trauma and abuse in your life, and you want to make sure there are no loopholes that will suck you back in. So you go to your trusted friend, Google. You browse through countless articles and videos about narcissistic abuse and before you know it, hours (sometimes days) have gone by, and nothing has been accomplished. In a semi-coma state, you finally give up because the only thing those dozens of blogs have said (aside from ranting on and on about how toxic and demonic narcissists are), is precisely what you already knew. There were no practical steps that could actually help. In fact, the only thing they accomplished was to make you more hysterical and dismayed. You probably needed to pop Xanax just to handle the overload, didn't you?

Well, you're not alone. Many of us try to seek answers on YouTube and blogs but eventually all that negative crap with no real solution causes us to want to give up. I don't want that to be your experience ever again. Here's a practical and straightforward technique to help you gain the sanity and freedom that's been taken from you.

It's a technique known as "No Contact," and I want to share with you exactly what it is, plus how to properly implement and maintain it so that you don't get sucked back into the web of narcissistic abuse.

What No contact is and what it isn't

This is the key that puts an end to the abuse. It locks the malignant narcissist out of your reality and puts an end to their manipulation and shenanigans. We use this technique to make sure the toxic person never again gets access to our emotions, our heart, mind, and spirit.

No contact isn't to be used lightly. It's not meant to be a trick or a game to get your narcissistic abuser interested in you again. Most people confuse No Contact with the silent treatment, so let's clarify that now.

The main difference between silent treatment and No contact is the intention.

Cults, churches, communities, and organizations have used silent treatment, aka cold shoulder, social rejection, isolation, or ostracism for centuries. It is a form of punishment or a way to inflict vengeance for a perceived wrong. The ancient Greeks are famous for using this technique to neutralize someone they considered a threat to the municipal or potential ruler.

In the corporate world, the silent treatment is usually a form of workplace bullying where the managers or supervisors punish the whistle-blower for carrying out unethical behaviors.

In a romantic or family setting, the silent treatment is more like an aggressive measure of control and punishment that narcissists love to use to motivate their victim into a particular behavior. I think silent treatment is the ultimate form of devaluation, and it causes victims to feel alone, neglected, voiceless, and invisible. In short, the silent treatment is a tactic favored by malignant narcissists and is usually used to manipulate you into doing things the way they want. It forces you to shut up and accept whatever crap they want to feed you, and it also allows them to play the hurt victim. No, this isn't anything close to what I want you to do for your healing because the intentions behind true No contact are very different.

With No Contact, you're not attempting to punish or bully anyone. In fact, it's not even about the abuser. This is about you protecting yourself and your reality. No Contact is implemented intentionally, deliberately, and its very nature is to break the cycle of abuse.

It should be used as a way to remove yourself from the influence of the toxic person so you can finally heal and transform your life for the better.

A significant component of healing yourself is being removed from the person and situation that wounds you. And as with all wounds, yours needs ample time to heal without being reinvigorated. By establishing no contact, you remove yourself from being a source of supply in that abusive and dysfunctional relationship.

Why we focus on remaining in No Contact

I know going No Contact is no easy task during the recovery process. However, you must give it your all because it stands as the crux that determines whether you will permanently heal and transform your life or remain a victim forever. The termination of an abusive, dysfunctional relationship usually leaves us feeling dead inside feeling unable to cope. Logically it made sense to terminate that toxic relationship because you know you don't deserve to be mistreated and taken advantage of, but emotions don't deal with logic. When you are madly in love with someone or in the case of having a narcissistic parent as your abuser, it's still hard to completely detach. Your emotions may hijack you and cause you to stray from the path of healing. As I mentioned earlier, while discussing trauma, the "trauma bond" that you form with your abuser will tend to keep you tethered to him or her even though you know it's not right. There's also other factors like feeling undeserving of true love, low self-worth, poor self-image, low self-esteem and co-dependency developed over time can actually keep you falling back into the web of abuse over and over again.

These reasons and so many other variables are the driving motives behind applying the no contact technique. You must create a space for healing, restoring, and rebuilding yourself from the negative influences of your abuser. No contact established the space for you to completely detach from the toxic person and move forward with your life. The more you're "out of touch" with the person both mentally, and physically, the easier it will be to retrain your mind, strengthen and control your emotions. You will be able to objectively look at the situation and relationship without having the malignant narcissist gaslighting you.

The more you practice no contact, the more resilient you become and are more capable of fighting the temptation to fall for the narcissists hoovering and manipulation tactics.

Here's how to apply No Contact immediately

Cut out all interactions and exchanges with the toxic person. That means not personal, virtual, or mental contact. You must remove and block your abuser from your phone, social media network, email, etc. Get rid of all triggers such as photos, gifts, or any other physical reminders that may trigger a memory of them. If the narcissist requests in any way shape or form to meet up immediately decline the offer.

This also means cutting them out mentally, which most victims forget to do. It's great to take physical measures to block the person from your life, but if you're spending most of the day thinking about, conducting conversations and arguments with the person in your head - then you're not practicing No Contact. You also need to avoid that urge to check on their updates through friends, social media, or other indirect ways. My best recommendation if you do have lots of friends in common with the abuser is to cut all contact with them too (at least as much as possible) and instead create a new support network that is separate and far removed from the influence of the malignant narcissist.

Following the examples and suggestions I have given on the subject of self-care practices, this should not be too hard to accomplish.

Let's talk about specific examples that you need to exercise your No Contact technique rigorously.

• If your narcissistic abuser made a key to your home without your knowledge and popped in to "check on you," flee the scene immediately. You can absolutely not engage them directly. The best course of action is No contact.

•If the narcissist doesn't have a key but still shows up to your home uninvited, do not answer the door. If they are still hanging around trying to get your attention to consider calling your local authority for help. Maintain no contact at all cost even if they brought a Mariachi band to serenade you.

• If you're walking toward your car from Yoga class or the weekly supermarket run and the narcissist appears from nowhere - make like the wind and drive away as fast as possible. Do not engage them in any conversation even if you want to yell at them for stalking you.

Sticking to your No Contact Rule

If you find yourself struggling to maintain No Contact with your abuser, consider scheduling your week with pleasurable activities that distract you. Get a massage, take long walks, read inspiring books, start a new hobby. Figure out a passion that you'd like to work on and devote as much energy as you can to that passion project. You can also integrate all the self-care tips that I offered. One great way of tracking and maintaining your progress as you implement this technique is to journal your thoughts daily. It can be a private journal, or if you're courageous enough, you can document the entire process as a blog journal. Where and how you do it doesn't really matter; what matters is that you find a safe outlet for your thoughts and emotions so they can stop hindering your progress. As you progress don't forget to celebrate your wins as well no matter how small. Both challenges and successful milestones deserve to be acknowledged as that is the path of healing and full recovery.

When a full No Contact isn't possible, what then?

Sometimes going No Contact just isn't possible. For example, if you have shared custody of the children or a legally binding business contract. In such cases, modified No Contact is the only solution to enforce so you can protect your emotions and allow healing to transpire. For many women divorcing their narcissistic husbands, things get really muddy when they get to this phase of recovery. If proper No Contact isn't carried out and the victim attempts to "stay friends" for the sake of the children she accomplishes many things none of which are healthy or progressive for her well-being.

This became really evident for Sheryl as she shares her story with us.

"I was in a 17-year relationship with my narcissistic abuser, 14 of those we were married. I ignored many red flags from the very beginning of our relationship, but his charm and love bombing were addictive. He caused me to lose not one but two professional careers, refused to move close to my family, and still, I stayed. After he retired, he left me alone for six months to work in a different state and refused to compromise. When he would get angry with me, which happened most of the time, he shouted, pushed me, called me names, slammed doors and would disappear from the house for hours just to punish me. He usually said, 'since you hate being alone, I'll make sure you stay alone forever.' Finally, I had enough and took some legal action this one time when we pushed me right after I had undergone surgery. But then a little while later he got sick and had to stay in the hospital for a while, so I decided to dissolve the legal action and help him out. He recently filed for divorce, and now I have lots of anxiety around this because I don't know if I can start over as my income is not what it should be. As I deal with the divorce I was trying to find a more amicable way of dealing with things and even suggested separation instead so that I can still keep my health insurance, I can see all it does is feed his already inflated ego. His adamant on getting this divorce and blames all our marital issues on me. I have to admit, I do feel guilty about some of the things I've said to him while angry and I know I keep bringing up the horrible things he's done to me which only makes him more furious but most of all, I wish I had the strength to leave sooner."

From that single example, it's clear to see avoiding No Contact with your abuser only enhances your suffering. It takes away your credibility for any boundaries or requests you make. You'll find yourself falling back when the narcissist needs extra "supply," and once they are done with you, they'll discard you yet again. Unfortunately, this enhances your feelings of self-loathing because you're holding out for a person who will never reciprocate your emotions, affections, or see value in you.

Therefore it goes without saying, No contact is the best solution. But if you can't do a full No contact, modify it with great caution taking extra measures to ensure your abuser is sealed off from your mind, body, and spirit. Remember, it is your birthright and responsibility to be happy, healed, healthy, and enjoy a good life. You don't have to prove to anyone (especially not the narcissist) that you are a good person. Leaving the lines of communication open or entertaining loopholes for them to get back in your head only delays your recovery and healing. Taking these extreme measures to cut all contact will be difficult and may even hurt in the beginning, but if you stick to it and keep forging forward, you will finally create healthy, empowering boundaries for your life that will enable you to thrive in all ways.

Chapter 10: 3 Steps To Reclaiming Your Power

By now, you are more than ready, educated, and equipped to begin your journey to healing and recovery. But there's one more life hack I wish to leave you with. You see, I believe that what we crave more than anything after going through abuse and trauma is to experience a sense of freedom and power. As victims of narcissistic abuse, we need to be able to do what we want, how we want, when we want, and we need to feel loveable again. Even if we remove the source of our pain, it's important we take measures to reignite that sense of freedom and power that was taken from us.

I know what it's like to be silenced, to feel invisible, unworthy, and undermined. That feeling of wanting to crawl into the deepest, darkest hole in the universe and just die there is all too familiar to me, and I know how hard it can be to break free from those old physical and psychological chains. In fact, after years of working on myself, I realize psychological chains are much stronger than physical chains. With everything, we've shared in this book, you now have a clear path to wholeness, truth, and incredible awareness. And there's one more thing you need to do for yourself to anchor yourself fully into the way of recovery.

It's a three-step process that will empower you to gain mastery over your emotions and reclaim personal power. The more of your personal power you can access, the faster and more permanent your recovery will be.

1. Take back your story and rewrite it.

Malignant narcissists are professionals at forcing false narratives on their victims. Unfortunately, we tend to buy into these fake stories and believe in them, which often places the abuser in the position of power. The fact that your narcissistic abuser is always right and you have no authority over what he or she says is a perfect example of this false narrative. As the abuser justifies the abuse, all you can do is affirm their perspective. Gaslighting is one of the ways narcissistic abusers feed their victims with false stories and negative self-perception.

Among the money false perceptions victims usually believe (for example, "you are damaged goods" or "you are not loveable") nothing is more harmful to the recovery process than carrying on the false self-beliefs and negatively charged trauma story.

By keeping the victim story alive and central to your life, you actually make it your whole life story, which continues to keep you in that same cycle. So now that your abuser is out of your life for good, this is your opportunity to rewrite the story of your life so that it can serve you as you rebuild your life. You cannot change the past or the pain you've had to endure, and you certainly cannot change your abuser. What you can change is the emotional charge and interpretation of the experience. I want you to undo the lies and manipulation through your own self-actualization and awakening. This will stretch you and won't necessarily be easy, but you must do it if you want to reclaim your personal power.

This doesn't mean going public with your story or anything that doesn't feel right to you. Instead, I want you to own this part of your life and perceive it as a chapter in your book of life. Whenever you look back at that chapter, I don't want you plunging back into pain and depression. So what are some things you can do to ensure that never happens?

A friend of mine who also grew up with an abusive parent decided to take this step seriously. He sat down one weekend with a journal and wrote down the story of his childhood in a manner that made him feel more empowered. Instead of seeing himself as a victim of abuse, he rewrote that chapter of his life depicting himself as a boy who learned very early in life to strong and independent thanks for the absence of his father. And his dysfunctional relationship with his mother was turned into a lifelong lesson on compassion and the understanding that not all mothers know how to express love in a healthy way. This in no way justified the hurt and trauma he'd experienced, but it did take the sting, resentment, and hatred out of his childhood memories restoring him to full power.

I invite you to reflect on your own trauma and pain. How can you take back your story and rewrite it so that in the coming months, years and decades you can look back with genuine compassion?

2. Forgive yourself.

I said it before, but it bears repeating here that forgiveness is one of the most powerful practices in recovery. Releasing the pain and trauma caused by your narcissistic abuser instead of choosing to hold on to it will help you heal faster. It's not easy, but it is possible to forgive completely. In a study in the Journal of Consulting and Clinical Psychology, Forgiveness Therapy showed the most promise as a way to overcome emotional trauma as compared to other forms of therapies. The control group that was treated using Forgiveness Therapy showed more significant signs of improvement over five years.

I want you to realize that you are not your past experiences, the emotions that usually torment you, and you are certainly not your mistakes. Feelings of guilt and shame must be eliminated from your mind. Acknowledge them when they show up, observe them without judgment, and choose to release them. You are not your thoughts or emotions. It is essential to your healing that you work on forgiving and accepting yourself unconditionally. Evict that internal voice that judges you all the time and instead practice the self-love and self-compassion practices that I shared earlier. The more you do this, the deeper your healing will be.

3. Rebuild your self-image and recognize your true worth.

I can't. I'm a failure. I don't feel worthy. I am weak. I'm unlovable must be replaced with new thought patterns and a new self-image. Repeat out loud right now the following: I can. I am succeeding in life. I am worthy of love and all good things. I am strong and confident. I am loveable. I love myself.

Let these thoughts be your new frame of mind. You must rebuild your self-image from victimhood to victorious. Challenge the inner dialogue and limitations that you notice inside your head. Get curious about your potential, who you really are, why you are here, and what purpose your life serves.

Louise Hay was a famous healer, metaphysical counselor and the founder of Hay House publishing (a company that has grown so much over the years that people like Wayne Dyer and Deepak Chopra published their books with her). She sold out countless seminars and trainings where she taught people how to do what she called "mirror work". An exercise in self-love where you'd look at yourself and speak words of truth and love until it becomes the new norm. What made Louise Hay so famous aside from her many books on self-healing was her unique story of triumph over devastating childhood trauma. Growing up she had a very dysfunctional childhood, experienced a lot of abuse and spent a big part of her life as a victim. In fact Louise Hay didn't recover and transform her life until she was in her 50s. In one of the recorded tapes that you can easily access on YouTube, she says that the words we speak and the thoughts we think about ourselves have more power than we know. They are the ones that keep us disconnected, stuck and in pain. It's not about what happened to you, it's about what you are doing now and the ideas you hold as true about yourself. There is no type of abuse or trauma you cannot recover from and Louise Hay did a good job proving it so.

Therefore, if you can find a way to tune into that power that lies within you, sustaining you at every moment - life will change for the better. You and I are not responsible for ensuring our bodies do the millions of things they do at each and every moment. I don't even know how my heart beats, and my lungs work, whether I am awake, asleep, angry, happy, or sad. The fact that the sun rises in the morning without fail, and winter always follows fall is a mystery too big to comprehend. We know life is bigger than us and yet we often get bullied into believing that we are helpless when that same power that makes that breathes life into birds and all the creatures of this planet is right here for us. Why not seek to understand how to access that same power that keeps the earth spinning on its own axis? Why not build an image of yourself that feels congruent with the grandeur and magnificence that is life itself? Why settle to be a second-class citizen of this planet when you are made of stars and have more power pumping through your veins than any human being can fathom?

You see the lies you've been fed all your life have caused you to experience this limited and lower version of life. But if you decide to stop accepting that BS and instead rewrite your story with what feels true to your core, you'd start to experience a completely new version of life. You will never outgrow your self-image because that is your perception of yourself. Malignant narcissists prey on their victims because most of the time, the self-image is distorted, and they can easily manipulate it. Now that you are here, it's time to work on forming a healthy self-image that no one can distort. It's time to define identity and value, not based on what people have told you before but because of the knowledge, understanding, and wisdom you've gained about the power that's breathing you. Until you become a child of this universe, people will always succeed in hindering your potential and value. Once you realize that you are powerful and loved beyond measure, then no one will be able to harm you.

Healing from narcissistic abuse is possible, and although it is very complex trauma, you can recover and rebuild your life. As victims of narcissistic abuse, we usually blame ourselves even without realizing it. Please stop it. Take your time with this process, see it more as a marathon than a sprint and go one day at a time if you must, but whatever you do, keep on the path of recovery. Know that being chained to the web of lies, manipulation, and abuse is not your fault. You are not broken and certainly don't need to accept a life of permanent misery. Although the abuse is part of your life's story, it doesn't and shouldn't be your whole story. Each phase of your recovery is essential, so don't skip over or try to shortcut the process. Understand that the journey is just as important as the destination. When times get really tough, that's okay too. Be in the present moment, soothe yourself as much as possible and keep reminding yourself that your new life isn't about striving for perfection; instead, it is abou progress. Your healing and transformation starts with one step. Take your first step today, and remember you are not alone.

Educational Resources

• Journal of Brian Behavior and Cognitive Sciences - http://www.imedpub.com/articles/the-cognitive-neuroscience-of-narcissism.php?aid=22149

• NPD test - https://barendspsychology.com/narcissistic-personality-disorder-test/

• The Gift Of Imperfection By Brené Brown - https://www.amazon.com/gp/product/159285849X/ref=dbs_a_def_rwt_bibl_vppi_i2

• Resource for grounding and soothing techniques - https://www.amherst.edu/system/files/media/Grounding%2520and%2520Self%2520Soothing%2520Techniques.pdf

• Louise Hay you can heal your life - https://www.amazon.com/You-Can-Heal-Your-Life/dp/0937611018